COMPANION GUIDE TO
Pope Benedict's
The Fathers

COMPANION GUIDE TO

Pope Benedict's
The Fathers

BY MIKE AQUILINA

Our Sunday Visitor Publishing Division
Our Sunday Visitor, Inc.
Huntington, Indiana 46750

Nihil Obstat: Rev. Michael Heintz
Censor Librorum

Imprimatur: ✠ John M. D'Arcy
Bishop of Fort Wayne-South Bend
November 10, 2008

The *Nihil Obstat* and *Imprimatur* are official declarations that a book or pamphlet is free from doctrinal or moral error. It is not implied that those who have granted the *Nihil Obstat* and *Imprimatur* agree with the contents, opinions, or statements expressed.

Excerpts from *The Fathers* copyright © 2008 by Libreria Editrice Vaticana and Our Sunday Visitor Publishing Division. All rights reserved.

The Scripture citations contained in this work are taken from the *Catholic Edition of the Revised Standard Version of the Bible* (RSV), copyright © 1965 and 1966 by the Division of Christian Education of the National Council of the Churches of Christ in the United States of America. Used by permission. All rights reserved.

Every reasonable effort has been made to determine copyright holders of excerpted materials and to secure permissions as needed. If any copyrighted materials have been inadvertently used without proper credit being given in one form or another, please notify Our Sunday Visitor in writing so that future editions may be corrected accordingly.

Our Sunday Visitor Publishing Division
Our Sunday Visitor, Inc.
200 Noll Plaza
Huntington, IN 46750

ISBN 978-1-59276-542-3 (Inventory No. T818)
LCCN: 2008940471

Cover design by Lindsey Luken
Interior design by Sherri L. Hoffman

Cover art:
The Evangelists of Cappadocia: St. Gregory of Nazianzus, St. John Chrysostomus, St. Basil the Great.
Museum, Antalya, Turkey
Photograph by Erich Lessing / Art Resource, NY

PRINTED IN THE UNITED STATES OF AMERICA

CONTENTS

INTRODUCTION   7

How to Use This Guide   7

Who Are the Fathers?   8

What Is a Father of the Church?   11

What Authority Do the Fathers of the Church Have?   12

What Is a Papal Audience?   12

Why the Fathers of the Church?   13

SESSION I: THE BEGINNINGS OF THE CHURCH   17

Chapter 1. *St. Clement, Bishop of Rome*   22

Chapter 2. *St. Ignatius of Antioch*   25

Chapter 3. *St. Justin, Philosopher and Martyr*   27

SESSION II: APOLOGISTS AND MARTYRS   29

Chapter 4. *St. Irenaeus of Lyons*   34

Chapter 5. *St. Clement of Alexandria*   36

Chapter 6. *Origen of Alexandria*   38

Chapter 7. *Tertullian*   40

Chapter 8. *St. Cyprian*   43

SESSION III: THE PEACE OF THE CHURCH   45

Chapter 9. *Eusebius of Caesarea*   48

Chapter 10. *St. Athanasius of Alexandria*   51

Chapter 11. *St. Cyril of Jerusalem*   53

Chapter 12. *St. Basil*   54

Chapter 13. *St. Gregory of Nazianzus*   56

Chapter 14. *St. Gregory of Nyssa*   58

SESSION IV: THE CHRISTIAN EMPIRE   61

Chapter 15. *St. John Chrysostom*   63

Chapter 16. *St. Cyril of Alexandria*   67

Chapter 17. *St. Hilary of Poitiers*   69
Chapter 18. *St. Eusebius of Vercelli*   71

SESSION V: ORDER IN THE MIDST OF CHAOS   73
Chapter 19. *St. Ambrose of Milan*   76
Chapter 20. *St. Maximus of Turin*   78
Chapter 21. *St. Jerome*   80
Chapter 22. *Aphraates, "the Sage"*   83
Chapter 23. *St. Ephrem, the Syrian*   84
Chapter 24. *St. Chromatius of Aquileia*   85
Chapter 25. *St. Paulinus of Nola*   87

SESSION VI: ST. AUGUSTINE   89
Chapter 26. *St. Augustine of Hippo*   92

INTRODUCTION

How to Use This Guide

When Pope Benedict XVI decided to give a series of audiences on the Fathers of the Church, he was doubtless hoping that millions of ordinary Christians would get to know those heroes of the faith better. This little book is intended to help achieve that goal.

Pope Benedict's talks are an excellent introduction to the Fathers. No one has more sympathy with the ancient Christan writers, and no one can bring them to life better. The Fathers may be separated from us by centuries, but they are still with us in their writings, and in that Communion of Saints we share with all the generations of the faithful. The Holy Father's talks can help us see these great Christians not as distant historical figures, but as old friends.

This book is designed to help you get the most from those audiences. You'll find background information, summary outlines of each audience, and questions to help you think about what the Pope and the Fathers have said.

We've divided the book into six sessions, and one good way to use it would be to make a six-week parish study group out of it. For study groups, it will probably be too much to try to discuss every one of the Fathers represented in a week's session. For that reason, we've picked out one "representative" Father for each session. That doesn't mean the one we chose is better than the others; it just means that his ideas, and the Holy Father's interpretation of them, seemed likely to provoke good discussions.

Of course, you can also use this book for individual study. We've provided summaries of the main points in each of the audiences, along with a few questions for reflection or discussion for each one. These are meant to be open-ended questions that make you think. There is no "right" answer to any of them, but you can always find a good starting point for an answer in the Holy Father's audience. For some suggested answers and/or guidance to the questions, go to Our Sunday Visitor's website (www.osv.com) and click on the "Books" tab followed by "Book Resources and Downloads."

The Fathers themselves constantly emphasize the importance of humility and prayer. Those are two things we need whenever we want to learn more about Christian history or the Christian faith. We need to be willing to learn, which means we need to be open to the possibility that we aren't always right about everything. And we need to ask for the Holy Spirit's guidance, because Christ promised us it would be there for anyone who asked.

Finally, we should be ready to enjoy ourselves. Learning about the Fathers isn't drudgery; it's an exciting adventure. We will come to know some of the most colorful characters in history, many of them great saints, but many of them also with charming quirks and eccentricities to remind us that they're human.

Who Are the Fathers?

The Fathers of the Church are those ancient Christian thinkers whose writings and thoughts have had the deepest influence on the doctrines of the Church.

The word "father" has always been full of meaning for Christians. The whole Christian Church is one family, so it's natural that we use the language of family relationships. Christ himself taught us to call God "Father," and we address the priests in our churches as "Father."

The word "Father" was used for Christian leaders from the beginning of the Church. St. Paul reminded the Corinthian church that he was their "father in Christ Jesus" (1 Cor. 4:15); St. John used similar language (3 Jn. 4). The men who inherited the Apostles' authority — the bishops they appointed — would have the same role in God's earthly family: they would be "fathers" to the Church.

Although every priest is rightly called "Father," when we speak of the Fathers of the Church, we mean a particular group of Christian men whose thought enriched the Church incalculably. That doesn't mean their words are infallible, like Scripture — in fact, we'll see that Pope Benedict has included a wayward thinker or two among the Fathers of the Church. But their witness is too important, and their influence on Christian thought too great, for us to ignore.

Because Christian doctrine has been passed down in tradition as well as in Scripture, the witness of the great teachers who came before us is always important, even vital. Even early on in the history of the Church, the bishops would often appeal to the precedents set by the "holy Fathers," the Christian thinkers who had come before them. The Apostles passed on what Christ had taught them, the next generation passed on what the Apostles had taught them, and so on.

When a bishop or a council made a public statement about a doctrine or practice, the statement would often refer to the precedents set by the "holy Fathers." The precedents were sometimes arranged in a "*catena*" (Latin for "chain") going all the way back to the Apostles, with a link for every generation in between. That way the teachers of the present could demonstrate that their own doctrine was the true doctrine that had been passed down uninterrupted and uncorrupted from the Apostles.

As time went on, the study of the Fathers became more important for defending the true Tradition of the Church against the challenges of the heresies. Everything having to do with the Fathers was preserved as carefully as possible. Some churches, like the Syrian city of Edessa, made great archives to hold the documentation of their own heritage. When the historian Eusebius (who is the subject of one of these audiences) was doing his research in the late 200s, he was able to make use of several collections like the one in Edessa. In the 300s and 400s, monastic communities also began to preserve the traditions of their "Fathers" in writing; and so we have inherited many anthologies of the lives and sayings of the so-called Desert Fathers.

Around the same time, at the end of the 300s, St. Jerome put together his book *On Illustrious Men,* which was a sort of biographical encyclopedia of ancient Christianity. With his profiles of individual writers, he included bibliographies, so we know what works were available to Jerome and can compare them to what remains all these centuries later. Like the history of Eusebius, Jerome's book became a standard reference for anyone studying the Fathers.

Not long after Jerome's work, in 434, Vincent of Lerins wrote a set of rules for studying the fathers that we call the "Vincentian Canon." Vincent, a monk from Gaul (now France), would one day be counted himself as one of the Church Fathers, and his guidelines are one of the foundations of Church theology.

> Now in the Catholic Church, we take the greatest care to hold that which has been believed everywhere, always and by all.... We hold to this rule if we follow *universality, antiquity,* and *consensus.*

We follow:

1. *universality*, if we acknowledge that one faith to be true which the whole Church throughout the world confesses;
2. *antiquity*, if we in no way depart from those interpretations that our ancestors and fathers clearly proclaimed;
3. *consensus*, if we keep following the definitions and opinions of all — or nearly all — the bishops and teachers of antiquity.

This is a good quick summary of what makes the Fathers of the Church so important. By studying what they had to say, we can know what the Church taught at various times, and what it has always taught throughout history. We know whether what we're teaching today holds to the rule of *universality*, *antiquity*, and *consensus*.

That knowledge becomes especially vital whenever the Church's teachings are questioned. In the Protestant Reformation, for example, Martin Luther and John Calvin never claimed to be inventing a new theology. They always said they were bringing back the ancient faith of the New Testament. They even pressed some of the Church Fathers into service to shore up their arguments.

But Luther, especially, would not take the Fathers on their own terms. He said they "often erred," and he knew — and acknowledged — that some of what he taught contradicted the consensus of the Fathers. Scripture was the only reliable guide, he said, and if his interpretation of Scripture contradicted what all his ancestors in the faith had said, Luther still preferred his own interpretation.

On the other hand, the Fathers themselves claimed to be passing on the interpretation of Scripture they had received from the Apostles. The argument, then, was about interpreting Scripture. Here is where the Fathers are a great help to us: they show us how the early Church really did interpret Scripture. If we want to know what the ancient Church — the Church that was closest to the time of the Incarnation — believed, then the Fathers can tell us.

For just that reason, reading the Fathers has often led Protestant scholars back to the Catholic Church. In the 1800s, John Henry Newman, an Anglican scholar, wrote that "the present communion of Rome is the nearest approximation in fact to the Church of the Fathers.... Did St. Athanasius or St. Ambrose come suddenly to life, it cannot be doubted what communion he would take to be his own." Shortly after he wrote those words, Newman followed the trail he had mapped out back to the Catholic Church.

In our own time, scholars and even ordinary readers continue to find their way to the Catholic Church through the Fathers. The witness of the Fathers is powerful — and the more you know about the history of the Church, the more powerful their witness is.

What Is a Father of the Church?

Broadly, the Fathers of the Church are the most important ancient Christian writers. Some early authors would use the word "Father" only to describe a bishop, but eventually the term was extended to priests (like Jerome) and laymen (like Justin).

Surprisingly, there's no official list. Theologians still don't agree completely. But there are four criteria that most theologians agree determine who should be called a Church Father:

1. sound doctrine
2. holiness of life
3. Church approval
4. antiquity

Ancient Christian writers who don't meet all these criteria are often described as "ecclesiastical writers" rather than Church Fathers.

Exactly how those criteria apply in any given case can provoke lively debates. Some of the figures are in no doubt whatsoever: every Catholic agrees that St. John Chrysostom and St. Augustine belong on the list. But questions arise when we encounter important Christian writers who strayed from the bounds of orthodoxy at one time or another.

Some scholars say that Tertullian, Origen, and Eusebius should be called "ecclesiastical writers" rather than Fathers, because they all dallied with unorthodox doctrines. Tertullian veered off into the Montanist heresy late in life, insisting that the Christians who had renounced the faith during the persecutions could never be forgiven and readmitted to the Church. Origen seems to have experimented with several weird theological notions. Eusebius was a bit too cozy with the most notorious heretics of the fourth century, the Arians.

Yet recent reconsiderations have been kind to those three men. The *Catechism of the Catholic Church* cites Tertullian explicitly as a Father of the Church (n. 1446) and nine times invokes Origen as an authority. Even if they had some wrong ideas, their contributions to orthodox Christianity are so vitally important that we simply can't ignore them.

For those reasons, Pope Benedict has included them in his audiences on the Fathers. You'll find one talk each on Tertullian and Eusebius, and Origen is so important that he deserves a two-parter.

What Authority Do the Fathers of the Church Have?

The *Catechism of the Catholic Church* often cites the witness of the Fathers. Pope Benedict has devoted a whole series of audiences to their lives and teachings. Even the Protestant reformers like Luther and Calvin heavily dotted their works with citations from the Fathers. It's hard to overstate how important the Fathers are in the development of Christian doctrine.

However, the works of the Fathers, unlike the books of the Bible, are neither inspired nor inerrant. And, unlike the popes, the Fathers do not teach infallibly. In fact, they often disagree with one another, and some of them didn't get along very well. St. Jerome argued against St. John Chrysostom; St. Jerome argued with St. Augustine; St. Jerome accused St. Ambrose of plagiarism. St. Jerome argued with almost everyone, as it turns out, and some of his opponents were themselves great Fathers of the Church — in the case of St. Augustine, at least, probably a more important voice in Christian theology even than St. Jerome himself.

But these arguments, spectacular though they sometimes were, don't change the fact that the areas of agreement are vast compared to the areas of disagreement. When there is a "consensus of the Fathers" on a particular doctrine or interpretation of Scripture, then the position of the Fathers must be held as true. The consensus shows us what has always been the teaching of the Church since the time of the Apostles.

What Is a Papal Audience?

Any chance to hear the Holy Father in the Vatican is called an audience, but the general audiences in this book were regular opportunities for the Pope to teach a large number of people at once. The first of the audiences on the

Fathers was given on March 7, 2007; the last audience on St. Augustine on February 27, 2008. There were audiences on some of the later Fathers after that, but St. Augustine was a convenient stopping point for the book.

General audiences are usually held on Wednesdays in the *Aula Paolo VI,* a large auditorium with a capacity of 12,000 people. Throughout the reign of Benedict XVI, the hall has consistently been full or nearly full.

The Holy Father can, of course, choose any subject he wants to speak about for these audiences. But since the time of Pope Paul VI, the audience talks have grown increasingly programmatic and theological in content. One of the best-remembered series of talks was Pope John Paul II's "theology of the body" series, which lasted several years and has already had a profound influence on Christian thought.

John Paul completed many series during his pontificate: on the Sacred Heart of Jesus, on the Psalms and canticles of the Bible, on religious life, and so on. Benedict has followed this model. His series on the Fathers follows his series on the Apostles and other figures of the New Testament, continuing the story of the early Christian Church. (See Our Sunday Visitor's book *The Apostles* by Pope Benedict XVI.)

Why the Fathers of the Church?

The Holy Father can choose whatever subject he likes for his weekly audience. Why would he choose to devote a long series of them to a group of ancient writers, many of whose names will be completely unfamiliar to most of his hearers?

Pope Benedict XVI is a good teacher. He knows that the way to make people pay attention is to talk about things they're interested in. And right now, the world is interested in Christian origins in a way it has hardly ever been before.

Books and movies like *The Da Vinci Code,* endless best-selling editions of Gnostic gospels, news stories about supposed tombs of Jesus and James, television documentaries about obscure heretical sects — the whole world seems to be fascinated by the origin of the Church, and everyone is asking some very sharp questions about it. How do we know which form of Christianity is really Christ's? Were the Gnostics the real keepers of Christ's teachings? Did the Catholic Church suppress the knowledge of the true teachings of Jesus in order to gain power for itself?

Against this background, we can begin to see the Holy Father's plan. We have a subject everyone seems to be interested in: Christian origins. Pope Benedict can use that interest to show us the truth about Church history. Although the talks we're studying are about the Fathers of the Church, the Holy Father's talks on the Fathers followed right after his talks on the Apostles themselves and the great figures of the New Testament. He's showing us how orthodox Christianity continues in an unbroken line from Jesus Christ through the Apostles through the Fathers of the Church to today. When we've heard the whole series, we'll know that the Church's claim to be the authentic repository of Christ's teachings isn't official "mythology." It's a documented fact of history.

That's what makes the Fathers so important. They are the ones who passed down the teachings of Christ and his Apostles, adding only what was in harmony with the original teachings to make them clearer and show how they applied to different situations. And with our fascination with Christian origins, the Holy Father can make use of the Fathers to show us how the Catholic Church has kept the true teachings of Christ down through the centuries. With this long series of audiences, we'll come to a correct understanding of Christian history, and we'll know that the wild stories we've heard from sensationalist would-be historians simply can't be true. The chain is unbroken, from Christ and the Apostles right down to us.

But there's more than apologetics behind the Holy Father's talks on the Fathers. The Fathers are still revered because of the power of their thought. Centuries after they wrote, their writings continue to inspire us and open our minds and hearts to the truth. Each one has a valuable contribution to make to our understanding of the faith we profess. With these talks, the Holy Father has a chance to bring the Fathers off their dusty bookshelves and into our lives. These are some of Pope Benedict's favorite writers; their thoughts helped form his faith. Surely it must give him great joy to be able to share them with Christian believers all over the world.

We can see some of that joy simply in the way the Holy Father delivers his talks. He has a prepared text in front of him, but people attending the audiences have often seen him simply lay down the text and speak to them extemporaneously. The published versions of his talks sometimes have to be compiled from transcripts of the audiences, since the prepared text is very different from the talk as he actually delivered it.

Introduction

It seems that the subject is very close to Pope Benedict's heart. What you'll read in his audiences on the Fathers, then, is the Holy Father's heart pouring out to you, hoping to fill your heart with a little bit of that love and enthusiasm he himself feels for the Fathers of the Church.

The Beginnings of the Church

The Christian Church was founded by Jesus Christ, who taught his disciples, who in turn passed down his teachings to their own disciples. In its first few decades, the Church grew enormously, but it was still a small part of the general population.

In this environment, many of the leaders of the Christians were men who had known the Apostles and had been personally taught by them. After the New Testament, we call the earliest generation of great Christian writers the Apostolic Fathers — the very early leaders who followed the Apostles themselves.

It was natural that the Apostles should raise up their most gifted students to be leaders like themselves. Jesus had left the Church in the Apostles' hands: their job was to teach what Jesus had taught and bring his message to the four corners of the earth. But they also had to manage the everyday affairs of the mushrooming Church — a job that got harder and more complicated as the Church mushroomed from a handful of believers to thousands of baptized Christians spread further and further through the ancient world.

To help with the teaching and the managing, the Apostles took their own most gifted disciples and made them leaders in the Church. As the Apostles died, these leaders took over, raising up disciples of their own to carry on the work.

The writings of the Apostolic Fathers are important for what they say, but they're also important for what they tell us about the earliest years of the Christian Church. These were men who had known the Apostles and had lived with them for years, hearing them teach and watching them at work. What they wrote is our window on primitive Christianity.

In turn, the leaders appointed by the Apostles also appointed leaders to succeed them, passing on the teaching of Christ in an unbroken chain.

Thus, early Christian writers are filled with a sense of personal closeness to the events of Jesus' life.

The World of the Early Church

The Apostolic Fathers and their immediate successors lived almost two thousand years ago. But in many ways their world was a place we can recognize.

The Roman Empire had taken over most of the known world, and the Romans did their best to standardize it. Just as today we see the same discount stores and fast-food joints wherever we go, Romans would find familiar architecture, customs, and language throughout the Empire. A Roman city in Britain was much like a Roman city in Syria.

In a world like that, people could move around a lot. Merchants traveled the length of the empire to buy this and sell that. Bureaucrats moved from posts in Spain to posts in Egypt without grumbling too much about it. With all that constant travel, a new idea could spread in weeks from one side of the world to the other.

Old traditions were breaking down, and people were always looking for something new. In place of the traditional gods, many Romans took up new esoteric religions imported from the East. The idea of sin and redemption — things the traditional Roman religion didn't take into account — seems to have been very attractive, and the popular new religions were the ones that promised a purification of some sort.

Most of these religions were tolerated, though the conservatives grumbled, because paganism was naturally tolerant. You have your gods, we have ours, and as long as you don't mind participating in the minimal rituals of the official religion, we don't mind what you do with your private devotions. An Isis worshiper did not deny the divinity of Jupiter; Isis was simply his favorite among the many gods in the religious shopping mall.

But Jews and Christians were different. They claimed that their God was the only God, and that all other gods were false gods. When they were required to make sacrifices to the Emperor's genius — his protective deity — they refused, saying that they could worship only one God. What was to be done with them?

Faced with the fact that the Jewish religion simply would not bend on this point, the Romans were usually very tolerant. Jews were exempt from most of the requirements forced on the other religions. But what about the

Christians? At first, they seemed to be nothing but a Jewish sect having some incomprehensible disagreement with the other Jewish sects. The Romans were used to multiple Jewish sects disagreeing with each other. But as the Jewish establishment began to make efforts to dissociate itself from the Christians, the Romans were forced to look at them as something else. And that something else had no right to exist.

To the Romans, what gave a religion its legitimacy was antiquity. The Jewish religion, however odd it might seem to the Romans, was very old. But if Christianity was, as some Jewish leaders were saying, a new religion, then it had no right to exist. No one had the right to make up a new religion.

The Christians did not think of themselves as followers of a new religion. Theirs, they believed, was the true religion of Abraham, Moses, and the Prophets. But they had a powerful incentive to distance themselves from the Jewish establishment when the Jewish revolt broke out in the 60s.

That revolt ended with the destruction of Jerusalem and the Temple in the year 70. For the Apostolic Fathers, the end of the Temple was the central event of their generation's history. The Old Covenant sacrifices ceased; the old world came to an end. Christianity and Judaism both had to come to terms with the fact that the center of the Jewish religion was gone. For Christians, it was a confirmation that the old order had passed away: the sacrifices are superfluous now, because we live in the age of the Messiah, who was himself the perfect sacrifice for all time.

With the rift widening between Christians and Jews, some Christian thinkers began to turn their efforts toward the pagans. Apologists like Justin wrote to pagan audiences to show how Christianity was philosophical and logical. Justin's principle was that everything good among the pagan philosophers was planted there by God and could usefully be adopted by Christians. As we'll see, Justin was proud of his education as a philosopher. Yet he also wrote for Jewish audiences, using all his skill in reasoning to show that Christianity was the true fulfillment of the Law and the Prophets.

Important Themes

The earliest Christian writers touch on almost everything that was important to the Catholic Church then and is still important today. But some distinctive ideas stand out.

1. *Living the Christian life.* The Apostolic Fathers emphasize over and over how important it is for the Christian to be a light to the world through his life, not just by what he says. Personal morality is one of the most important concerns for a Christian.

2. *The organization and discipline of the Church.* The structure of the Church was established by Jesus himself, but it was the Apostolic Fathers who had to work out the fine details of it. As early heresies arose, the leaders of the Church had to decide, based on what Christ and the Apostles had taught them, how to deal with false teachings and threats to Christian unity.

St. Clement wrote to the church in Corinth to sort out an ugly dispute that had seen the established leaders of the congregation thrown out and replaced with younger men whose reputations were at best not yet formed. To deal with the problems, he had first to establish — in the gentlest possible way — his authority as Bishop of Rome, and then to lay down the principle that the order of the Church is sacramental, rather than just political. The leadership descends from Christ himself through the Apostles. It is not simply a convenient style of management, to be changed when we don't find it convenient anymore; it is ordained by Christ as the order for his family on earth.

3. *The Eucharist.* Already, the Apostolic Fathers show a strong sense of the Eucharist as the center of Christian life. To Christians who think of sacramental theology as a later innovation, their Eucharistic sense of the Church can come as a surprise. But readers of the Acts of the Apostles may recall that the very earliest Christians devoted themselves to "the breaking of bread" from the very foundation of the Church (see Acts 2:42).

4. *The freshness of the Incarnation.* Some of these writers may have seen Jesus in person; many (if not all) of them had learned from people who knew Jesus. To them, the Incarnation was recent news, not history. Their writings constantly remind us that Jesus' career on earth was a living memory. In fact, the apostle John was still alive when St. Clement was Pope. The Christian faith was based on the personal experience of God's coming to dwell among us.

Representative Father

If you can read or discuss only one of the audiences, read the one about **St. Clement, Bishop of Rome** (Chapter 1). All the topics that concerned the Apostolic Fathers come together in Clement's Letter to the Corinthians, in which Clement explains to the troubled people of Corinth that living the Christian life is inseparable from the proper organization of the Church.

In Practice

Work on humility this week. Just start with the little things in your own family and with your friends. Let someone else shine brighter in the conversation. Don't insist that you know best even when you're an expert. Try to think of all the things you've argued about that you could have just let go. Then, after you've worked on that for a while, if you have problems with some of what the Church teaches, make an honest effort to understand why the Church teaches that way.

More to Read

For an introduction to the Apostolic Fathers, read *The Fathers of the Church, Expanded Edition*, by Mike Aquilina, pages 53-54. See also *The Fathers* by Pope Benedict XVI, pages 7-23. (Both of these books are available from Our Sunday Visitor.)

CHAPTER 1

St. Clement, Bishop of Rome

If there is one dispute St. Clement is most often brought in to settle, it's the question of the primacy of Rome. Already in the generation that knew the Apostles, Clement's *Letter to the Corinthians* shows the leadership in the Church of Rome writing to a church in another great city as if Rome had the authority to regulate the affairs of Corinth. For that reason alone, it's a tremendously important document — it shows that the idea of Roman primacy was not a late invention, but one that went right back to the beginnings of Christianity.

Yet in the early Church, Clement's letter was famous not so much for settling that question as for the wisdom and love Clement displayed in writing it. Clement is concerned with the order of the Church, and he wants the disputes in Corinth to be settled as soon as possible — but not because he enjoys exercising authority and wants to extend his power. On the contrary, the way to unity is through humility and charity. Living the Christian life is the most important thing: let everyone do that, and arguments about authority will disappear.

Main Points

1. Clement was fourth Bishop of Rome, heir of Peter.
2. He had known and been taught by the Apostles.
3. Clement's letter to the Corinthians demonstrates Roman primacy over the other churches in the very earliest days of the Christian Church.
4. Humility and charity will restore unity.
5. The order of the Church is sacramental rather than political.
6. Secular government is a legitimate institution, but it too is responsible to God.

Questions for Reflection or Discussion

1. Clement writes to the Corinthians as if he had authority to settle their disputes. When is it necessary for a Christian leader to assert authority rather than attempt to persuade his flock?
2. Why does Clement argue from the example of the Old Testament temple rituals in Jerusalem?
3. How does the structure of the Church correspond to the message of the Gospel?
4. Why does Clement need to point out that the first bishops were appointed by the Apostles?

From St. Clement's *Letter to the Corinthians*, 41-42

Order is essential in the Church. St. Clement uses the example of the Old Testament sacrifices to show that everything has its place in the Church, and every Christian has a particular function in the Body of Christ.

Let every one of you, brethren, give thanks to God in his own order, living in all good conscience, with becoming gravity, and not going beyond the rule of your own kind of ministry. The daily sacrifices are not offered everywhere, brethren — or the peace-offerings, or the sin-offerings and the trespass-offerings — but only in Jerusalem. And even there they are not offered just anywhere, but only at the altar before the temple, and the offering is first carefully examined by the high priest and the ministers. So anyone who does anything beyond what God wills is punished with death. You see, brethren, that the greater the knowledge given to us, the greater also is the danger to which we are exposed.

The apostles have preached the Gospel to us from the Lord Jesus Christ; Jesus Christ has done so from God. Christ therefore was sent forth by God, and the apostles by Christ. Both these appointments were made in an orderly way, according to the will of God.

So when they had received their orders, and had been fully assured by the resurrection of our Lord Jesus Christ, and established

continued on next page...

in the word of God, with full assurance of the Holy Spirit, they went forth proclaiming that the kingdom of God was at hand.

And thus preaching through countries and cities, they appointed the first-fruits [of their labors], having first proved them by the Spirit, to be bishops and deacons of those who should afterwards believe. Nor was this anything new — indeed, it was written a long time before about bishops and deacons. For Scripture says somewhere, "I will appoint their bishops in righteousness, and their deacons in faith" [compare Is. 40:17].

CHAPTER 2

St. Ignatius of Antioch

Martyrdom hangs over every word we read from St. Ignatius, because when he wrote his letters, he knew he was being taken away to die. He rejoiced in the knowledge: he would be given what he considered the greatest possible gift, to be united with Christ in suffering.

That impending union with Christ gives Ignatius's thought a crystalline clarity. He has only a certain time left in this world; he must focus on what is truly important. And above all, what is important to him is that the brothers and sisters he leaves behind should live in unity. It seems appropriate that Ignatius is the first writer to use the word "catholic" (meaning "universal") to describe what the Church ought to be.

He urges the ordinary believers to be submissive to their bishops and pastors. The hierarchical structure of the Church is necessary to keep Christians together. But it is a hierarchy of love. As Pope Benedict points out, the hierarchy is not opposed to the fundamental equality of Christians. On the contrary, the hierarchy is exactly what makes that equality possible.

Main Points

1. St. Ignatius was the third Bishop of Antioch, the city where the name "Christian" was first used.
2. On his long journey toward martyrdom, St. Ignatius stopped at churches throughout Asia Minor, warning them against heresies and divisions.
3. Unity, says St. Ignatius, is vital for the Church.
4. This unity is expressed in faithful submission to the hierarchy of the Church.

Questions for Reflection or Discussion

1. Why does Ignatius resist being rescued from martyrdom? What makes martyrdom so desirable to him?

2. What effect do you think his approaching martyrdom might have on St. Ignatius's advice in his letters?
3. How does the Trinity give us the pattern for Christian unity?
4. How do we know whether we are promoting or impeding unity in the Church?
5. What does the church in Rome have to do with Christian unity?

CHAPTER 3

St. Justin, Philosopher and Martyr

Throughout Christian history there has been a tension between two schools of thought on the subject of the Church's engagement with secular thought. One extreme says that Christianity is complete in itself: Scripture and Tradition tell us all we need to know, and secular philosophy or science has nothing to do with it. The other extreme says that the best way to understand and explain Christianity is through the terminology of science and philosophy.

Neither extreme is exclusively right. God revealed the truth to us, but he did so in many ways. Scripture itself appeals to our reason in the wisdom books, to our hearts in the books of poetry. There is no one correct way to come to an understanding of the truth.

Justin was educated as a classical philosopher and proudly wore his philosopher's uniform. But he applied his logic to explaining the Christian faith. He believed that any truth to be found in philosophy was only one part of the great Truth that is Christ the Word. Scripture leads us to Christ, but so does reason. As he said (probably infuriating the pagan philosophers), "whatever things were rightly said among all men are the property of us Christians." Not surprisingly, then, Pope Benedict presents Justin to us as a model for Christian participation in the intellectual life of current culture. He was the most important of the early apologists — writers who argued the case for Catholic Christianity.

Main Points

1. St. Justin was famous as an apologist, one who defended the Christian Church and explained its doctrines.
2. He looked for truth in classical philosophy and applied that philosophical training to Christianity when he converted.
3. For Justin, the truths found in philosophy are parts of the universal Truth that is Christ.
4. Both reason and Scripture lead to Christ.

Questions for Reflection or Discussion

1. Does modern science lead us toward Christ?
2. Does knowing about secular philosophy or science make us better evangelists?
3. If all branches of knowledge are part of Christ, how does that change the way we think about what we know?
4. How does Christianity clarify all the other knowledge we have?

Apologists and Martyrs

After the work of the first generations of great Christian thinkers, it was no longer possible for Rome to ignore the Christians. But what could they make of Christianity? What had at first seemed like an insignificant Jewish splinter group was more and more looking like something different. What was it?

Officially, Christianity was an illegal cult. If it was not the Jewish religion, as many Jews insisted it was not, then it did not have the antiquity that made Judaism respectable, or at least tolerable, in Roman eyes. And its beliefs seemed bizarre and possibly dangerous, especially filtered through popular rumor. Christians did not allow the unbaptized to participate in the Eucharist, the central mystery of their religion. No one who was not already baptized could even see what happened there. But rumors circulated that it involved eating flesh and drinking blood. The Christians must be cannibals! Wild stories spread about Christians kidnapping pagan children for their horrible cannibal feasts.

Heresies, which had already sprung up in the time of the Apostles, began to take firm root in the time of the Apologists. Some of these heresies erred in being too rigorous: there were those, for example, who would refuse ever to forgive any Christian who had denied the faith during an anti-Christian pogrom. Others went in the opposite direction, erring as libertines; they argued that the body was only a prison for the soul, and therefore whatever the body did was unimportant.

Obviously, the Catholic theologians had their work cut out for them. On the one hand, they had to counter the effects of rumor and ignorance and show the pagans that their religion was both ancient and reasonable. On the other hand, they had to face down threats from within, explaining to Christians themselves why the orthodox faith was the true teaching of Christ.

Even as great thinkers were beginning to tackle the more difficult questions of theology, the Roman government was growing more fearful — and more intolerant — of the new Christian religion. The age of apologists was also an age of martyrs.

We shouldn't think that the Romans always killed every Christian. Like most totalitarian governments, the Romans weren't very efficient. Since Nero's time, the law had said that Christianity was illegal, but most of the time pragmatic Roman policy worked under a "don't ask, don't tell" rule: officials were told not to go looking for Christians, arresting only the ones who made too much of a spectacle of themselves.

Because of this policy, the Christian leaders — bishops especially — were the ones most likely to suffer in ordinary times.

The average Christian could just live an average life, but a Christian leader's job was to make it obvious that he was a Christian. Not surprisingly, the strong possibility of martyrdom meant that only the most enthusiastic and persuasive Christians became leaders in the Church.

The Roman powers thought it would be easy to eliminate the Christian cult by eliminating its leaders. It worked with any other cult the Romans decided to attack, because other cults were top-down affairs, and they made no claim to exclusivity. You could worship Isis and still make offerings to Jupiter; that was fine with both. If the temple of Apollo closed, you could still go to the temple of Mercury and have somebody up there on your side.

But the Christian religion was exclusive, and it was built on the foundation of the unwavering belief of its members. They could not accept any other god, and they could appoint bishops as fast as the government could kill them off.

The result was that the Christian religion continued to grow, and famous martyrs only encouraged the ordinary believers. And most of those believers could live most of their lives unmolested.

Every once in a while, something stirred up the simmering hatred of the new cult, and a full-blown terror would result, with ordinary Christians rounded up and executed by hundreds or thousands. Persecutions rose and fell like tides, and every few years another one would break out, testing the resolve of the Christians and making more heroic martyrs to strengthen their faith.

Mob violence was also always a real possibility. Christianity spread to the big cities first, and even when there was no official persecution, hysterical mobs might be whipped into a frenzy by dark rumors of Christians practicing human sacrifice.

But still, most Christians lived most of their lives in peace — though always with the fear that they might be taken away, and always with the heroic examples of their leaders who had died for the faith.

In fact, it would be hard to imagine a better environment for the growth of a new faith. Martyrdom selected the most inspiring leaders; their heroic firmness strengthened the faith of the Christians and converted many pagans; and the number of Christians continued to swell until they were threatening to take over the Empire.

In fact, even as the last of the persecutions was raging, the historian Eusebius was already writing his history of the Church. By that time, persecuted or not, the Church must have seemed like an unstoppable ocean liner charging full steam ahead.

Important Themes

The earliest Christians had concentrated on advising and encouraging the Christian believers and had begun reaching out to the pagans to show them that Christianity was not at all unreasonable. Now we begin to see a more sophisticated approach to theology, one made necessary both by the opposition of philosophical pagans and by the distinctions in doctrine that separated Catholic Christianity from the increasing number of heretical sects.

In writers of this period we see longer, more carefully reasoned arguments. In addition, the threat of martyrdom always hung over Christian writers in this era, and that gave them a strong focus on strength and faith.

1. *Arguments that Christianity is reasonable.* Like Justin, some writers turned to the traditional vocabulary of classical philosophy to show that Christian doctrine not only was not against reason, but in fact was more reasonable than the many conflicting popular schools of philosophy.

2. *Arguments that Christianity fulfills the Old Testament prophecies.* For Jewish audiences, the argument is that Christianity is the true faith of Abraham, Moses, and the prophets. To Tertullian, this was the only argument. He rejected Justin's beloved Athenian philosophers: "What does Athens have to do with Jerusalem?"

3. *Arguments for orthodox Christianity against various heresies.* Among the Apologists of the day were some who became famous as heresiologists —

the most famous being Irenaeus, who attacked heresy with reason and devastating wit.

4. *Sacramental martyrdom.* Following St. Paul, Christian writers often saw their own sufferings as a kind of Eucharistic offering. In martyrdom, a Christian carried the imitation of Christ to its logical conclusion: actually participating in his suffering and death. "I am the wheat of God," St. Ignatius of Antioch wrote. "Let me be ground by the teeth of the wild beasts, that I may be found the pure bread of Christ."

5. *Encouragement in fortitude.* Naturally, Christian writers devote much of their writing to encouraging their fellow Christians in the face of persecution and death.

6. *The institutional Church.* In spite of the persecutions, and indeed because of the persecutions, the Christian Church was still growing at an astonishing rate — one sociologist estimates its growth at 40 % every ten years. It was now a gigantic institution spanning the entire Empire — almost a shadow government, in fact. Christian writers of the time were dealing with the newly institutional character of the Church, working out the details of its organization and administration.

Representative Father

If you can read or discuss only one of the audiences in this section, read the one on **Tertullian** (Chapter 7). His influence on Christian thought is still incalculable, and his life — even his drift into heresy — epitomizes the struggles of the Church in this age of turmoil.

In Practice

You may not be called to die for the Christian faith. Very few of us are these days. But Jesus Christ still calls us to take up our crosses and follow him.

What is your cross? What witness is God calling you to bear to the world? Look around you. It may be right next to you; you may be bearing your cross already. But make a special effort to ask yourself what you should be doing to make your own life an inspiring example of Christian faith.

More to Read

For more about this period in the history of the Church, you can read *The Fathers of the Church, Expanded Edition*, by Mike Aquilina, pages 73-74. See also *The Fathers* by Pope Benedict XVI, pages 24-56. (Both of these books are available from Our Sunday Visitor.)

CHAPTER 4

St. Irenaeus of Lyons

St. Irenaeus is most famous for cataloguing and refuting dozens of heresies that were already making the rounds in his time. In many cases, his notice of them is all we have left of certain obscure Christian splinter groups. It was a work that tested the patience of a saint, and every once in a while he would burst out in a fit of sarcasm when he encountered a particularly ridiculous belief. But the rock on which his argument rested was always the knowledge of the Apostolic Tradition. What had been passed down from Christ through the Apostles to their successors was the true Christian faith, not made-up doctrines that came from unbridled philosophical speculation.

Main Points

1. Irenaeus probably learned from Polycarp, who learned from the Apostle John.
2. He catalogued and refuted Christian heresies.
3. The Gnostics, a diverse category of heretics who believed that there was some secret Christian knowledge available only to the elite, were one if his main targets.
4. Irenaeus opposed *dualism,* the belief that matter is evil because it was created by an evil creator opposed to the will of God.
5. For Irenaeus, the Apostolic Tradition is the guarantee of the truth of the Christian religion.
6. The Spirit of God dwells in the orthodox Christian Church.

Questions for Reflection or Discussion

1. Why is the Apostolic Tradition important in determining which is the true doctrine of Christianity?
2. How do we know which tradition is truly Apostolic?

3. How do we judge today whether a doctrine is truly Apostolic or simply a human invention?
4. What is the role of Rome in keeping the Apostolic Tradition safe from corruption?

CHAPTER 5

St. Clement of Alexandria

The whole idea of knowledge was controversial among Christians in St. Clement of Alexandria's time. The Greek word for knowledge, *gnosis,* had been appropriated by the Gnostics, a group of loosely related heretical sects. What the Gnostics had in common was a belief that there was a secret knowledge, a *gnosis,* that only the elite could have. They used (and abused) the language of Greek philosophy to write endless ponderous speculations on the origins of the universe, sometimes claiming that their increasingly bizarre inventions were secret doctrines passed on from Christ to one of his disciples (Thomas was a favorite candidate).

Orthodox Christian thinkers sometimes reacted by rejecting classical philosophy altogether: "What does Athens have to do with Jerusalem?" Tertullian famously asked.

But Clement of Alexandria took a different approach. For him, Greek philosophy was a tool that could be used to explore and explain the truths of Christian theology. Philosophy purified the soul and made it ready to receive the Truth. There was a true Christian *gnosis:* God can be known by those who love him.

Main Points

1. St. Clement had a strong interest in classical philosophy, which he applied in his thinking on Christian doctrine.
2. True knowledge comes from reason guided by the Truth that is Jesus Christ.
3. Knowledge of Christ is love.
4. The purpose of life is to become like God.
5. Good works and knowledge of the Truth are inseparable.

Questions for Reflection or Discussion

1. How does the knowledge of Christ that we gain through the Church guide our reason?
2. If the purpose of life is to become like God, what's the difference between us and the people who built the Tower of Babel (see Genesis 11)?
3. How is Clement's idea of *gnosis* different from the Gnostic idea of secret knowledge available only to the elite?
4. How is love different from the passions from which Clement says we must be free in order to be a "true gnostic"?

CHAPTER 6

Origen of Alexandria

Origen is a difficult character among the Fathers. He was Christianity's first real speculative theologian, and sometimes his speculations drifted outside the bounds of sound doctrine. But he always desired to be united to the Catholic Church. Though he sometimes made mistakes, he was not a heretic: he never intentionally taught any false doctrine.

The dry and technical prose of Origen's writing gives little hint of the passionate, almost fanatical Christian he was in life. His father was martyred when Origen was seventeen years old; Origen would have gone to present himself to the authorities at the same time, except that his mother had hidden his clothes, preventing him from leaving the house.

Eventually, after an extraordinarily productive career, he was imprisoned and cruelly tortured. From the effects of that torture he died, earning his martyrdom at last. Since then his reputation has sometimes been dubious, but recent years have seen a sort of Origen revival. Pope Benedict considers him so important that he has devoted two audiences to Origen.

PART 1. LIFE AND WRITINGS
Main Points

1. Origen's father was martyred when Origen was seventeen years old, setting an example he always remembered.
2. Origen's desire for martyrdom colored his faith and his life.
3. His theology rested in a careful reading of Scripture.
4. The "literal" sense of Scripture is the ordinary meaning of the words.
5. The "moral" sense is the lesson we derive from Scripture about living our own lives.
6. The "spiritual" sense is the sense in which Scripture speaks of Christ.
7. Origen thus is one of the chief promoters of the Christian interpretation of the Old Testament.

Questions for Reflection or Discussion

1. How does the way we live influence what people hear when we tell them the Good News about Jesus Christ?
2. Martyrdom is very unlikely for most Christians in our circumstances. How can we translate Origen's desire for martyrdom into the way we live our own lives?
3. Why is the Old Testament still important to Christians? Hasn't the New Testament replaced it?
4. The Bible is a great library of sometimes difficult books. How do we know when we've interpreted the Bible correctly?

PART 2. TEACHINGS

Main Points

1. Prayer is one of Origen's main themes, and for him prayer is even more important than study for a knowledge of the Scriptures.
2. Love of Christ is the only way to a real knowledge of Christ.
3. The priesthood belongs to all believers in Christ: we are a "priestly race" and must make ourselves holy as priests.
4. Each one of us is capable of making the priestly sacrifice on the altar of God by taking up the Cross and following Christ.

Questions for Reflection or Discussion

1. Why is prayer absolutely essential for a proper understanding of Scripture?
2. How can the love of Adam for Eve be compared to the knowledge of Christ?
3. How is Origen's experience of Christ like human love between a man and a woman? How is it different?
4. If we the lay members are also priests, how can we exercise our priesthood when we have ordinary jobs and family responsibilities that take up all our time?

CHAPTER 7

Tertullian

Tertullian was an extraordinarily talented man; his one deficiency was that he perhaps neglected the virtue of charity. He demanded high standards of others, as he did of himself. But sometimes his standards were just too high.

When persecutions against the Christians erupted, most Roman officials tried to be reasonable and humane. All the accused had to do was offer the proper sacrifice to the Emperor's genius, and all the charges would be dropped.

Of course, a Christian could not in good conscience offer a pagan sacrifice. But when the alternative was torture and a gruesome death, many Christians took the easy way out.

When the persecution had passed, many of those Christians who fell away would naturally feel ashamed of themselves, and many of them wished to rejoin the Church. The official policy was that their apostasy could be forgiven if they undertook exemplary penance. But there were some Christians — and Tertullian was one of them — who could never bring themselves to forgive the Christians who had lapsed. They had committed the one unforgivable sin, these extremists argued: they had blasphemed the Holy Spirit.

Rather than forgive those who had fallen, Tertullian and his followers ended up separating themselves from the Catholic Church. This is the great blemish on Tertullian's reputation: he fell into heresy because he just could not stand all that Christian forgiveness the Catholic Church was doling out.

Nevertheless, Tertullian's work is much more wheat than tares. His immeasurable contribution to Christian theology trumps his heretical intransigence to earn him a place among the Fathers of the Church.

Main Points

1. Tertulian was an African who was the first important Christian writer in Latin.

SESSION II: Apologists and Martyrs

2. He drifted into the Montanist heresy, which refused forgiveness to Christians who had fallen away during persecutions.
3. "The blood of Christians is seed"; martyrdom only spreads the faith rather than discourages it.
4. Tertullian clarified the doctrine of the Trinity: one substance, three Persons.
5. Humility is the essential virtue of the theologian; Tertullian failed in humility.
6. Nevertheless, his contributions to orthodox Christian theology cannot be ignored, in spite of his later heresy.

Questions for Reflection or Discussion

1. What examples of martyrdom inspire us today? Does martyrdom necessarily involve physical death?
2. How do we commit the same errors Tertullian did? How can we avoid them in the future?
3. Is a form of the Montanist heresy still alive in our Church today?
4. When a theologian separates from the Church, how can we sort out what's valuable in his or her thinking from what is in error?

From Tertullian, *Apology,* 50

Tertullian tells the pagan persecutors why their tortures and murders will only create more Christians. The blood of Christians is seed: everyone who sees the fortitude of the martyrs is impressed, and many end up becoming Christians themselves.

But go on with zeal, good presidents. You will be more popular if you sacrifice the Christians as the people wish. Kill us, torture us, condemn us, grind us to dust — your injustice is the proof that we are innocent. Therefore God suffers that we thus suffer.

For only just recently, in condemning a Christian woman to debauchery ("*leno*," a pimp) rather than to the lions ("*leo*"), you confessed that we consider a taint on our purity more terrible than any punishment and any death.

continued on next page...

Nor does your cruelty, however exquisite, do you any good. It is rather a temptation to us. The more often we are mown down by you, the more of us there are: *the blood of Christians is seed*.

Many of your writers exhort us to bear pain and death with courage, as Cicero in the *Tusculans*, as Seneca in his *Chances*, as Diogenes, Pyrrhus, Callinicus. Yet their words do not find so many disciples as Christians do — Christians who are teachers not by words, but by their deeds. That very stubbornness you rail against is the professor. For who can see it without asking what is at the bottom of it? Who, after finding out what is at the bottom of it, does not embrace our doctrines? And who, when he has embraced them, does not desire to suffer so that he may partake of the fullness of God's grace, that he may obtain from God complete forgiveness, by giving in exchange his blood? For that secures the remission of all offenses. This is why we give thanks right on the spot for your sentences. Since the divine and human are always opposed to each other, when we are condemned by you, we are acquitted by the Highest.

CHAPTER 8

St. Cyprian

St. Cyprian was a great admirer of Tertullian, but he could not bring himself to be as unforgiving as Tertullian was of Christians who had broken down under persecution. In North Africa, the persecutions had been especially fierce, and many Christians broke down under torture. Tertullian and his followers, like the Montanists, said that those Christians had committed the unforgivable sin against the Holy Spirit. But Cyprian insisted that the Church could always receive the truly penitent.

Cyprian himself never renounced Christianity, but he avoided martyrdom when he thought he was still needed, even going into hiding during one persecution. But eventually there came a time when he had a choice between apostasy and death. He chose death. In that way he showed that he had high standards for himself, even though he was willing to forgive others who couldn't meet those standards.

Main Points

1. Cyprian had to shepherd the church of Carthage through two terrible persecutions.
2. The question of what to do about Christians who had fallen away during the persecutions divided the community.
3. Cyprian steered a middle course, requiring exemplary repentance before the fallen ones could be brought back into the Church.
4. He insisted that the Church was one, founded on Peter.
5. Outside the Church, Cyprian said, there is no salvation.
6. Prayer is the work of the heart, not merely of the lips.
7. But Christians pray together even when they pray in private, because all Christians are one in the Church.

Questions for Reflection or Discussion

1. How do we fall away from the Church today? Do we face persecution even in our comfortable churches?
2. What sort of repentance do we offer for our failings?
3. How do we pray with the whole Church even when we pray alone?
4. If we remember that we are standing in God's sight, how does that affect the way we pray?

The Peace of the Church

The whole world changed when the emperor Constantine, readying himself for a battle that would decide the fate of the western Empire, adopted the Christian religion. Having won the battle, Constantine proclaimed the Edict of Milan, granting religious freedom throughout the Empire.

For the first time in history, freedom of religion was the official policy of a great world power. Although Constantine's descendants would revoke this edict and start persecutions of their own against the pagans, Constantine deserves the credit for being the first world leader to impose religious freedom as a matter of public policy.

Historians still debate whether Constantine's conversion was a sincere religious experience or a cold calculation. By his time, in spite of recent heavy persecution, Christians were the largest single religious group in the Empire. Constantine was battling other claimants to the throne: it certainly would be handy to have numbers on his side.

On the other hand, once he adopted Christianity, Constantine seems to have shown a sincere faith, and Eastern churches revere him as a saint.

Though every religion theoretically had the same rights, Constantine heavily favored the Christians. From a persecuted underground movement, Christianity suddenly emerged as a state-supported institutional Church.

But the new freedom gave Christian heresies the chance to come out of the shadows, too. Heresies had grown up even while the Apostles were still alive, and they continued to multiply and divide throughout the times of persecution. Now they were free to preach their own sometimes bizarre interpretations of Christianity. Naturally, orthodox Christians condemned their teachings, but the heretics condemned the orthodox right back. The Peace of the Church was quickly turning into the most contentious era in ecclesiastical history.

The arguments got so fierce that Constantine himself was alarmed. In the East, especially, it was perfectly possible to stir up a riot in the streets by discussing a controversial point of Christian doctrine. That made the theological debates not just an embarrassing breach of Christian unity but a threat to state security as well.

Constantine decided something had to be done. He called the bishops of the Church together for a great meeting at Nicea, and told them to work out their differences.

Much Church business was discussed at the Council of Nicea. Delegates worried over mundane issues like providing a system of wayside hostels for Christian pilgrims. But the heresies, and especially the Arian heresy, dominated the discussions.

Arius was a bishop who taught that Christ was not equal to the Father. Christ was truly the Messiah, but he was created in time; he occupied a place intermediate between God and God's creatures.

The Council of Nicea rejected Arius's doctrines and formulated the first version of the Nicene Creed we recite today — the creed that is so specific about Jesus Christ's being "God from God, light from light."

But the Arian heresy didn't go away. In a pattern that will be familiar to anyone who watches the theological controversies of today, Arius and his followers managed to persuade themselves that the Council of Nicea had not said anything they couldn't agree with. Yet they continued to teach that Jesus Christ was a lesser being, not truly of one being with the Father. Constantine himself was sympathetic with the Arians, and more pragmatically he just wished the whole controversy could be smoothed over politely. He didn't care so much who won as that the Empire should be at peace, and the orthodox bishops seemed so unreasonable in their insistence that only one doctrine could be right. It wasn't long before some of the orthodox bishops found themselves on Constantine's enemies list.

The figure of Athanasius towers over this era. Staunchly orthodox and always ready for a fight, Athanasius was exiled over and over from his see in Alexandria, returning only to have trouble stirred up against him again by the Arians and their sympathizers. Athanasius was uncompromising and infuriatingly intelligent, and he especially annoyed Arians who couldn't match his arguments. Today his unwavering commitment to the faith of the Apostles has made his name practically synonymous with orthodox Christian doctrine.

Important Themes

1. *The divinity of Christ.* The Arian heresy was the biggest challenge facing the orthodox Church, and the writers of the time had to address it.

"We do not worship a creature," Athanasius wrote. "Far be the thought. For such an error belongs to heathens and Arians. But we worship the Lord of Creation, Incarnate, the Word of God."

2. *The divinity of the Holy Spirit.* Refuting the arguments of the Arians forced the orthodox theologians to examine and refine what they had always believed about the Trinity. Athanasius was the first to write a treatise on the divinity of the Holy Spirit.

3. *Monasticism.* At a time when the Church was going through its first real period of worldly prosperity, many faithful Christians were feeling the urge to withdraw from the world. St. Anthony was collecting followers at his desert retreat, and once again it was Athanasius who wrote a biography of his friend Anthony and spread his ideals throughout the Empire.

Representative Father

If you can read only one of the audiences in this section, read the one on **St. Athanasius of Alexandria** (Chapter 10). His career encapsulates the period in miniature: the Catholic Church, finally freed from three centuries of persecution, forced once again to defend itself, but this time against heretics from within its own ranks.

In Practice

What are you doing for Christian unity? It's a serious question, and it will take some serious thought to answer. Have you put a lot of effort into trying to understand the Catholic doctrines that seem most difficult to you? Do you understand the main points of difference between Catholic beliefs and the beliefs of, for example, your Protestant friends? What unites us as Christians is far greater than what divides us, which makes it all the more important for us to try to understand those small but vitally important points of division. Real progress toward unity can begin only when, like St. Athanasius, we've thoroughly understood both sides.

More to Read

For more on this period in the history of the Church, you can read *The Fathers of the Church, Expanded Edition*, by Mike Aquilina, pages 121-122. See also *The Fathers* by Pope Benedict XVI, pages 57-100. (Both of these books are available from Our Sunday Visitor.)

CHAPTER 9

Eusebius of Caesarea

Eusebius was the first great historian of the Church. Even during the last great persecution, he was already putting together his history. When Constantine adopted Christianity and decreed religious freedom throughout the Empire, it seemed to Eusebius that God himself had chosen Constantine to rule over God's kingdom on earth. The history he wrote turned into a history of how God directed events to lead to the ultimate Christianization of the Empire.

Instead of a divine peace, however, the Christian Empire quickly polarized into Catholic and Arian factions. Eusebius was not interested in what he regarded as esoteric theology; he thought everyone should just get along, and proposed a compromise that didn't satisfy anyone. When the imperial authorities turned against Athanasius and his followers, Eusebius joined the persecution of the orthodox side, whom he must have seen as intransigent troublemakers.

But in spite of his sympathy with the Arians, Eusebius's history is simply our most valuable source for knowledge of the first three centuries of the Church. He had access to archives and records that have long since disappeared, and he was a careful researcher, citing his sources and quoting them at length.

Main Points

1. Eusebius was the first historian of the Church, but also one of its great philologists. (A philologist is someone who studies the origins of words.)
2. For Eusebius, the Apostolic Succession is the backbone of Church history.
3. History reveals the love of Christ for his Church, in spite of persecutions and heresies.
4. Eusebius's history is Christocentric: it puts Christ at the center.

5. For Eusebius, the study of history is not just idle curiosity but a way of coming to know and love God.

Questions for Reflection or Discussion

1. Why is it important or even useful to know the history of the Church?
2. How does the succession from the Apostles help us make sense of Church history?
3. Do we still see the love of Christ working in his Church in modern Church history?
4. If Christ is at the center of our history, how does that help us understand what's happening to us now?
5. How can even the recent history of the Church lead us to know and love God better?

From Eusebius, *Church History,* Book II, Chapter 3 "The Good News Spreads Far and Wide"

Whenever Eusebius speaks of the spread of the Cristian faith, he never forgets to give the main credit to God himself. The Apostles and their successors were the earthly instruments of evangelization, but it was God working through them that brought about the good results.

So, under the influence of heavenly power, and with God's help, the doctrine of the Savior, like the rays of the sun, quickly lit up the whole world. And immediately, just as it says in the divine Scriptures, the voice of the inspired evangelists and apostles went forth through all the earth, and their words to the end of the world.

In every city and village, churches were quickly established, filled with crowds of people, like a threshing-floor filled up with grain. And those whose minds were, because of the errors they had learned from their ancestors, held captive by the ancient disease of idolatrous superstition, were set free by the power of Christ working through the teaching and the wonderful works of his disciples — liberated,

continued on next page...

you might say, from terrible masters, and released from the cruelest bondage. With disgust they turned their backs on every kind of devilish polytheism, and confessed that there was only one God, the creator of all things. And they honored that one God with the rites of true piety, through the inspired and reasonable worship that our Savior has planted among us.

CHAPTER 10

St. Athanasius of Alexandria

Athanasius was a stubborn man at a time when stubbornness was exactly what was required. It would have been easy to compromise with the Arians — to accept Eusebius's formula, for example, which attempted to be vague enough to satisfy both sides. But Athanasius would not compromise the truth.

It was Athanasius whose insistence on the divinity of Christ carried the day at the Council of Nicea. But the Arians stubbornly refused to give in, even after the Council had reached its conclusion. The authorities, including Constantine himself, were concerned mostly with peace and tranquility; Athanasius cared only that he was right. To Constantine, he seemed like a hotheaded fanatic, a troublemaker who threatened the peace of the Empire. He was sent into exile, and for the next few years he would be repeatedly called back to his see of Alexandria and sent into exile again, as fashions in theology changed among the ruling powers.

But Athanasius never wavered in his insistence on the truth of the Catholic faith. Today his name is almost synonymous with orthodox Catholic Christianity; in fact, the churches of the East call him the Father of Orthodoxy.

Main Points

1. Athanasius was the pillar of orthodoxy in a difficult time.
2. The Arian heresy threatened to supplant orthodox Christianity in Athanasius's time.
3. Against the Arians, Athanasius held that Christ was truly God, and that therefore God himself was accessible to Christians.
4. St. Anthony, the founder of monasticism, was Athanasius's friend and inspiration, not for his theology but for his exemplary life.

Questions for Reflection or Discussion

1. Why is it important to remember that St. Anthony, who wrote no books of theology, was St. Athanasius's friend and inspiration?
2. Unity was vital to all the early Church Fathers. How do we balance working for unity with defending orthodoxy?
3. What dangerous heresies might St. Athanasius be battling if he were on earth today?
4. Most of us are not famous theologians. How can we follow St. Athanasius's example?

CHAPTER 11

St. Cyril of Jerusalem

St. Cyril was exiled three times by the Arians for his orthodoxy, and yet he was suspected of having Arian sympathies by many orthodox Catholic bishops. It was a hard time to be cautious and reasonable, which were two of Cyril's outstanding qualities.

But Cyril was a great teacher. His catechetical lectures are models of their kind, poetic, precise, and perfectly composed — even though he spoke extemporaneously. We have them today only because at least one of his students furiously scribbled notes.

Main Points

1. Cyril was known both for his exemplary pastoral care and for his taking part in the Arian controversy.
2. Cyril's writings as a teacher were most famous.
3. His catecheses take new converts through the basics of the faith into the mysteries of the Sacraments and on into the life of prayer — the whole Christian rebirth through Baptism.
4. They involve body, mind, and spirit, setting a pattern for effective catechesis in the Christian Church.

Questions for Reflection or Discussion

1. How would Cyril's exemplary pastoral care for his flock affect his catechesis?
2. How would it affect the arguments he made in the Arian controversy?
3. Cyril's catecheses were delivered in the Basilica of the Holy Sepulcher, built over what was believed to be the tomb where Jesus' body was laid. How would the surroundings have affected his listeners?
4. Why would a bishop famous for engaging in theological controversies devote so much of his effort to teaching the very basics of the faith?

CHAPTER 12

St. Basil

Like many of the best early Christian writers, St. Basil was brought up with the best classical education. He came from a family of saints, but for the first few years of his adult life he seems to have been more interested in worldly success than in Christian holiness.

That changed dramatically with a sudden conversion experience. He had been a successful teacher of rhetoric; now he abandoned all his worldly goods and became a hermit.

His reputation for outstanding holiness and equally outstanding teaching soon attracted a crowd of followers, and the hermit Basil had almost by accident become the head of a monastery. Later he was made bishop of his home town, Caesarea in Cappadocia. As bishop, he was a tireless and effective administrator, which is all the more remarkable because the Arian controversy necessarily occupied so much of his attention. He always preferred gentle persuasion to fiery confrontation, but he made enough enemies anyway. Arian emperors tried to force him to see their point of view, but he stared them down and — amazingly — was left alone to work himself into an early grave.

PART 1. LIFE AND WRITINGS

Main Points

1. St. Basil was known for his exemplary holiness.
2. Although he was born into a family of saints, he went through a personal conversion experience in which he rejected worldly success in favor of the truth of the Gospel.
3. He balanced his good works with solitary prayer and meditation.
4. Basil turned monasticism outward, making the monastery a fountain of life to the community around it.
5. He made important contributions to the doctrine of the Trinity.

Questions for Reflection or Discussion

1. Is it necessary for even someone raised as a Christian to go through a conversion?
2. Why would Basil think it was necessary for monks who had devoted their lives to prayer and contemplation to go out and do good works in the community?
3. On the other hand, why was it necessary for those good works to be rooted in prayer and contemplation?
4. Why would someone so interested in charity be so concerned with the proper celebration of the liturgy?
5. How might Basil's devotion to charity affect his theology of the Trinity?

PART 2. TEACHINGS

Main Points

1. The three Persons of the Trinity are all equally God.
2. That God himself died on a cross for us tells us that human beings have great dignity.
3. We are responsible for one another; we are stewards of whatever goods God gives us, which are to be used for helping others.
4. Frequent Communion gives us the power to live the Christian life.
5. Whatever is good in pagan writers can be used with benefit in educating Christians; we should participate critically in the culture of the day.

Questions for Reflection or Discussion

1. If human beings have great dignity, how does that affect how we live a Christian life? Why should we be mindful of our greatness?
2. Why did Basil give so much importance to the subject of possessions? How does knowing that what we possess really belongs to God affect what we do with it?
3. Why such frequent Communion? How does the Eucharist help us in living the Christian life?
4. How do we engage with the culture of today? What from our own popular culture might St. Basil adapt to Christian ends?

CHAPTER 13

St. Gregory of Nazianzus

The childhood friend of St. Basil, St. Gregory of Nazianzus never really wanted to be a leader in the Church. When his friend Basil more or less accidentally founded a monastery, Gregory went there to live a secluded life of contemplation. But his ailing father, a bishop, called him home and insisted on ordaining him a priest. He resented the intrusion on his pleasant solitude, and he entered on his priestly duties reluctantly.

He was still more reluctant to be made a bishop, but it happened anyway. Just as reluctantly he went to Constantinople, the imperial capital, to argue the apparently losing orthodox side in the Arian controversy. As soon as he had the opportunity, he retired from active Church life and the politics he found so distasteful, spending his last years on his family estate praying and writing.

PART 1. LIFE AND WRITINGS
Main Points

1. Gregory devoted himself to solitude and meditation.
2. He accepted his ordination with reluctance, but put Providence before his own wishes.
3. He used sharp reasoning and clear logic to defend orthodox theology against the Arian majority in Constantinople.
4. For Gregory "the Theologian," theology is not pure reason, but comes from a life of prayer and holiness.

Questions for Reflection or Discussion

1. Is God calling us to some duty in the Church that we may not wish to take up? How do we distinguish God's call?
2. How can we tell when going against the majority isn't also going against God's will?

3. Do our Christian beliefs ever lead us into unseemly hatred, lies, and division? How can we remedy those things without abandoning the defense of what's right?

4. Was Gregory wrong to abandon his episcopate in Constantinople when the opposition grew too strong? Or is there a time when fighting for what's right is worse than walking away?

PART 2. TEACHINGS

Main Points

1. Gregory was mild and peace-loving, but prayed to overcome his timidity when necessary.

2. Charity is the way of salvation, because charity brings us all together as one in the Body of Christ.

3. Prayer is necessary for everything in life.

4. The true purpose of life is finding God, for whom we long just as God longs for us.

Questions for Reflection or Discussion

1. Is natural mildness like Gregory's a gift or a curse to be overcome?

2. How does the doctrine of Mary as "Theotokos" flow from the doctrine of the Trinity, which Gregory so zealously defended?

3. If we are really "one in the Lord," why are some of us richer or healthier than others? Why are there obvious differences in the family of Christ?

4. If our true task is to find God, why do we spend our time doing good works instead of studying Scripture and contemplating the mysteries of theology?

CHAPTER 14

St. Gregory of Nyssa

St. Gregory of Nyssa was the younger brother of St. Basil, and his life followed a similar course. He also taught rhetoric, but gave it up and joined Basil in Basil's monastery. Basil ordained him a priest and then Bishop of Nyssa, a see in Armenia. Arians dominated in Nyssa, and they had little use for Gregory. To add to the troubles, Gregory was not much good as an administrator. He was tossed out of his diocese for financial mismanagement.

From then on, Gregory distinguished himself as one of the leading theologians of his day. He took the best of classical philosophy, notably Plato's works, as a framework for his own profound works of mystical and systematic theology. In the East, his theology was so influential that the Second Council of Nicea (680-681) called Gregory the "Father of Fathers."

PART 1. LIFE AND WRITINGS
Main Points

1. St. Gregory continued the work of his brother St. Basil in defending the orthodox faith from heresy.
2. All his work in theology and the defense of the orthodox faith was in the service of one goal: to discern what was truly worthwhile.
3. Creation was one of his favorite subjects, especially what it means for man to be made in the image of God.
4. By purifying ourselves of sin, we can rise to the dignity of our original creation and see God, which is our goal in life.

Questions for Reflection or Discussion

1. Why did God give us rule over every other creature? What does it mean to say that we are kings over creation?
2. How does that affect the way we deal with the world around us?
3. What are the responsibilities of a king?

4. Many heretics denied the goodness of creation. Why is it so important for orthodox Christianity to affirm the goodness of creation, even though our sin has tainted it? Why would creation be such an interesting subject to a defender of the orthodox faith?

PART 2. TEACHINGS
Main Points

1. Our goal is to make ourselves like God.
2. God created us in his image: because we have the likeness of the divine in our own souls, we can find God within ourselves.
3. A life of holiness is true fulfillment, and detachment from the evils of this world is a necessity for ascending to God.
4. Charity for the poor is also essential, because in the poor we should see Christ.
5. Finally, nothing can be accomplished without prayer.

Questions for Reflection or Discussion

1. Why does Gregory dwell so much on the dignity of man and our special place in creation? How is that different from pride?
2. If creation is good, why do we need to detach ourselves from the things of this world in order to rise up to God?
3. If we need to detach ourselves from the things of this world, why must we pay special attention to the poor instead of just ignoring them?
4. Why do we need prayer if charity is the ladder to heaven?

The Christian Empire

The controversies of the Nicene period trained a new generation of theologians: deep thinkers who were ready to explore the subtlest implications of the Christian faith. At the same time, the memory of the martyrs was still fresh, and the burning faith of the early centuries was still a bright flame.

The Roman Empire was officially Christian now, with Christian emperors and a Christian government. Paganism still survived here and there, especially in rural areas — in fact, the word "pagan," the name Christians used for people who still stuck to the old religion, comes from the Latin word for a country-dweller. But when the emperor Julian "the Apostate" tried to revive the ancient Roman religion, he didn't get very far, and Julian himself died with the words "You win, Galilean" on his lips.

It should have been a period of peace and prosperity for the Church, but instead it was a period of strife and controversy. The Council of Nicea was supposed to settle the Arian question once and for all, but the Arians managed to ignore it, or to claim that their doctrines were somehow compatible with the conclusions of the Council. Other heresies flourished as well, and the orthodox theologians were kept busy either arguing their case or going into exile and coming back again.

Some of the great figures of Christian thought lived in this era. St. John Chrysostom (his nickname "Chrysostom" means "golden-mouthed") especially stands out. He preached sermons that reach across the centuries and stir us from our creaky pews today.

The foundations of the Church had been laid long before, but these were the thinkers who began to build Christian theology into a magnificent cathedral, filled with beautiful and intricate detail, but every detail a part of the harmonious whole.

Important Themes

1. *Systematic theology.* Augustine and others attempted to organize all the strands of thought left to them by the Fathers before them, putting

everything together into a system of theology that would serve the Church for the rest of time.

2. *Orthodoxy.* As heresies continued to flourish, even finding support from the imperial government, Catholic Christian thinkers were called on to defend the orthodox doctrine and to make their positions clear. The result was more and more refinement of the orthodox doctrine — more precise definitions, and a firmer understanding of exactly what Catholic Christians believe.

3. *Christian morals.* In the days of persecution, being a Christian had been costly. You could pay for it with your life. But when the government was actively encouraging Christianity, and beginning to discourage paganism, it was easy to be a Christian, or at least call yourself one — often easier than not being Christian. Many nominal Christians lived as though they had never heard of Christian morality. Over and over, we hear Christian leaders exhorting their flocks to live the faith they profess to believe in — to give up immorality, to love the poor instead of trampling on them.

Representative Father

If you have time for only one of the Fathers in this group, read the audiences on **St. John Chrysostom** (Chapter 15). The story of his life encapsulates the story of the period, and his marvelous preaching still inspires conversions today.

In Practice

In spite of occasional opposition in popular culture, it's easy to call ourselves Christians today. But are we living Christian lives? Try to imagine what someone like St. John Chrysostom would tell us about the way we live. Then try to imagine how we might follow his advice.

More to Read

The life of St. John Chrysostom is also told briefly in Aquilina, *The Fathers of the Church, Expanded Edition*, pages 177-179. See also *The Fathers* by Pope Benedict XVI, pages 101-128. (Both of these books are available from Our Sunday Visitor.)

CHAPTER 15

St. John Chrysostom

"Chrysostom" means "golden-mouthed" in Greek, and his nickname gives us a good idea of his place among the Fathers. His thinking was profound, and his theology was orthodox; but it is his inspiring speaking and the beauty of his expressions that we remember above all.

John's homilies to his flock in Antioch were full of concrete examples that hit home — everyday problems from everyday life, with practical Christian solutions to real challenges that everyone faces.

His reputation spread far and wide, and in 398 he was named patriarch of Constantinople, the imperial capital. It was about the last thing he wanted to do, but the emperor sent armed soldiers to bring John back with them, so there was no question of refusing.

In Constantinople, John's program of moral reform earned him many enemies, including the empress Eudoxia, who played a starring role in some of John's pointed homilies on vanity. John's enemies succeeded in having him exiled, but the ordinary people of Constantinople nearly revolted, and Eudoxia herself had to call him back. Still John did not rein in his golden mouth, continuing to preach against vanity and excess. Once again he was exiled, and when his sermons still managed to find their way back to Constantinople he was sent still farther away. Weakened by forced marches, he died en route.

When news of his death reached Rome, the Pope and the Western Church excommunicated all those who had persecuted John, refusing to restore communion until they had repented. John's body was brought back to Constantinople, and the new emperor himself came out to meet the coffin and beg forgiveness for his mother Eudoxia.

PART 1. THE YEARS IN ANTIOCH
Main Points

1. St. John Chrysostom was raised by his Christian mother after his father died when he was a child.
2. He wished to live a contemplative life, but reluctantly accepted the call to be a leader in the Church.
3. Above all, he was famous for his eloquent preaching.
4. It was vital for him that true doctrine be matched with a truly Christian life.
5. Christian marriage and family life are among his favorite themes.

Questions for Reflection or Discussion

1. How might growing up without a father have affected St. John Chrysostom's view of family life?
2. Is it better to be a leader in the Church than to live a contemplative life in solitude?
3. How could his years of withdrawal from people and public life prepare St. John to be a leader in the Church?
4. Why would knowing correct doctrine be important for leading a truly Christian life?

From St. John Chrysostom, *Letter to Olympias* "Read My Letters and Console Yourself"

St. John Chrysostom often suffered exile for his tenacious orthodoxy. Here he writes to a friend who was feeling depressed, urging him to read his letters and remember that anything he can suffer in this world is a tiny price to pay for glory in the next. Nothing we suffer here is real suffering: only sin is distressing.

I have already sent you three long letters: one by the proconsular soldiers, one by Antonius, and the third by Anatolius my servant. Two of them were a healthy medicine that could revive anyone who was desponding or stumbling, and bring him into a healthy state of serenity.

continued on next page...

When you have received these letters, then keep going over them thoroughly, and you will see their force and feel their healing power, and you will feel better, and you will let me know that they have done you much good.

I have a third letter ready, too, similar to these, which I do not choose to send right now, because I was really vexed when you said, "I keep thinking sorrowful thoughts, even inventing problems that do not exist." It is not worthy of you to speak that way. It makes me hide my head for shame.

But read the letters I have sent, and you will no longer say things like that, even if you are completely determined to be despondent. I have always said, and always will say, that sin is the only thing that is really distressing, and that everything else is only dust and smoke.

For why should we grieve about going to prison and wearing a chain? Or about being ill-treated when we gain so much by it? Or why should exile grieve us, or confiscation of goods?

These are just words. They have no terrible reality; they are words without sorrow. For if you speak of death, you're only talking about the debt of nature: something you have to go through eventually even if no one brings it sooner. And if you speak of exile — well, that's only a change of country and a bit of sightseeing. Or if you speak of confiscation of goods, that's only freedom and emancipation from care.

PART 2. THE YEARS IN CONSTANTINOPLE
Main Points

1. As Bishop of Constantinople, St. John Chrysostom lived austerely, making sure the poor were well taken care of and that the liturgy was celebrated magnificently.
2. Knowledge of creation is a ladder by which we can rise to knowledge of God.
3. God also gives us Scripture to complete our knowledge.
4. More than that, God himself descends to dwell among us, and sends his Holy Spirit to dwell in our hearts and transform us.

5. The primitive Church is a pattern for a new model of society, in which the primacy of the person is foremost.

Questions for Reflection or Discussion

1. If St. John wanted to help the poor, why did he celebrate the liturgy with such magnificence? Wouldn't that money be better spent on the poor?

2. Why can't we know God through creation alone? Was creation defective in some way so that it had to be supplemented by Scripture?

3. What pattern does the primitive Church give us for society? How should we change our thinking about what society should be?

4. If the primitive Church is the pattern for society, what should we do about our secular government? Should we be trying to foment a revolution?

CHAPTER 16

St. Cyril of Alexandria

St. Cyril was successor to Athanasius as Patriarch of Alexandria, and like his predecessor he was a famous champion of orthodox Christianity. But the challenge had changed a bit. A new heresy, perhaps a little more subtle than the Arian heresy, had taken over at Constantinople.

Nestorius and his followers taught that Mary could not truly be called "Mother of God," as the Church had traditionally called her. God came before Mary; therefore she was not Mother of God. Cyril did not condemn Nestorius without thoroughly investigating the question, repeatedly asking Nestorius to clarify points. But Nestorius got stubborn and a bit arrogant.

Eventually, Nestorius asked the emperor to call a council of the church to settle the question. At the Council of Ephesus in 431, Cyril's orthodox formulation prevailed over Nestorius's innovations — much to the joy of the common people, who had never been willing to give up their enthusiastic devotion to Mary.

Main Points

1. St. Cyril is known as the "seal of the fathers" for his unwavering commitment to the tradition passed down through the Fathers from the Apostles.
2. He fell into conflict with Nestorius when Nestorius taught that Christ's human nature was separate from his divine nature.
3. Cyril insisted on the orthodox doctrine that the divine nature and the human nature of Christ are inseparably united, so that it is proper to call Mary "Mother of God."
4. The very same Son who was begotten before time was also born of the Virgin Mary.
5. Although he insisted on true doctrine, Cyril also worked to find a statement of that doctrine that all believers could accept.

Questions for Reflection or Discussion

1. The controversy with Nestorius seems abstract and intellectual. Why was it so important both to Cyril and to the ordinary believers of his time?

2. If Cyril knew what the true doctrine was, why did he compromise about the wording? Where is the line between compromise and caving in?

3. The Holy Father has spent his whole life studying the most complicated theology. Why does he say that the faith of the People of God is "a guarantee of sound doctrine"?

4. Cyril made "shrewd alliances" to gain the condemnation of Nestorius. Is that kind of politics really becoming to a Christian? (See Mt. 10:16 for more to think about.)

CHAPTER 17

St. Hilary of Poitiers

Hilary was probably a convert from paganism. He had learned classical philosophy in the approved manner, but he found the truth in the Bible that he had never been able to find in philosophy.

It was a difficult time to be a Catholic. The Arian heresy had the support of the Emperor, and while Hilary's province of Gaul (modern France) had remained mostly orthodox, the Arians were using their political might to force their theology into the province. When Hilary resisted, the emperor exiled him to far-off Phrygia in Asia Minor.

It was a bit of a mistake for the Arians. They dominated Phrygia, but Hilary had such a reputation for clear thinking and Christian charity that he earned the respect of influential people there. Finally the Arians begged the emperor to send Hilary back to his diocese in Gaul so that he wouldn't make any more trouble in the East. The same Catholic faith that exiled him had sent him home. For the rest of his life he lived at peace in his diocese of Poitiers.

Main Points

1. St. Hilary devoted his career to defending the orthodox faith.
2. His most important work was *On the Trinity*, in which he showed that Scripture clearly witnesses the divinity of the Son.
3. His whole Trinitarian theology is developed from the baptismal formula given us by Christ: "In the name of the Father and of the Son and of the Holy Spirit."
4. Although he tenaciously opposed Arianism, a "spirit of reconciliation" is characteristic of Hilary: he sought out points of agreement with those who had not yet arrived at the truth and used those points to lead them to the fullness of faith.
5. The unity of the Trinity is a necessary consequence of God's complete love.

Questions for Reflection or Discussion

1. Why does Hilary begin his exploration of the Trinity with the formula for baptism?

2. Can we find points of agreement with people who oppose us today? With, for example, Protestants, Jews, Muslims?

3. How do we know when we have compromised too much in looking for points of agreement?

4. How can we, like Hilary, combine gentleness with strength in dealing with problems in our own parish?

CHAPTER 18

St. Eusebius of Vercelli

One of the most obscure of the Fathers of the Church, St. Eusebius of Vercelli is known only from a few surviving writings and a bare outline of his life. He has, however, a personal connection to the Holy Father. As Joseph Ratzinger, the future Pope Benedict XVI was once titular Archbishop of Vercelli, and thus a direct descendant in office of St. Eusebius of Vercelli. This meditation on a relatively neglected Father of the Church is a small payment on the debt the Holy Father owes to his holy predecessor.

Main Points

1. Eusebius was known for setting a memorable example of self-denial in governing his diocese.
2. He was inspired by St. Athanasius's *Life of St. Anthony* to found a monastery-like priestly community in Vercelli.
3. He was exiled for defending orthodoxy against the Arians, but returned in the reign of the indifferent Julian the Apostate.
4. He and his clergy lived like monks in the middle of the city.
5. This self-denial was a constant reminder that permanent value is not in the things of earth, but in Christ.

Questions for Reflection or Discussion

1. How do self-denial and defending orthodox doctrine go together?
2. Is it necessary to live a monastic life in order to stay focused on heavenly things?
3. How could we follow Eusebius's example of self-denial in our everyday lives?
4. Who are our spiritual predecessors in our own parishes and neighborhoods? What examples have they left us to follow?

Order in the Midst of Chaos

Outside, the world was falling apart. "Barbarians" — tribes of foreigners who didn't speak Latin or Greek — were overwhelming the once-mighty Roman Empire, an Empire that had seemed like something ordained by God to be coextensive with the Christian faith. In the year 410, barbarian Goths overran the city of Rome itself, a city that had not seen a foreign invader in centuries.

The remaining pagans blamed the Christians for turning the people away from the old gods. The Christians struggled to understand what was happening to them. They were forced to remember that, however temporarily prosperous they had been in the Nicene era, this world was not their true home. Riches in this world are temporary; only wealth laid up in heaven is secure.

All the ingredients came together to produce a generation of the most profound and most memorable Christian writers in the history of the Church. Names like St. Ambrose, St. Jerome, and St. Augustine fill the footnotes in catechisms and theology textbooks. But they're also loved by millions of ordinary Christians. St. Augustine wrote one of the most moving autobiographies of all time, a book that still makes readers weep and shout for joy. St. Jerome translated the Bible into the common Latin of the people, giving the church a reliable version that's still the basis for the official Latin translation.

In the end, the Roman Empire in the West fell to pieces, and Western Europe split into dozens of squabbling little kingdoms. The only remaining force for order was the Church, faithfully preserving the knowledge and culture passed down by the Fathers until the world was ready for them again.

Important Themes

1. *The duty of the Christian citizen.* As the Empire fell apart, the Church was more and more the only organization capable of keeping any

order at all. Bishops had to remind their flock that a good Christian must exercise the civic virtues. In the present danger, it was even more important that good Christians should be good citizens.

2. *Christian charity.* Bishops constantly had to remind their flocks that the present troubles were not an occasion for greedy profiteering, but that there was an even greater need for charity. Christians who were still prosperous had a duty to share their goods with those who had nothing.

3. *The Arian heresy.* In spite of the Council of Nicea, which was supposed to settle the matter once and for all, the Arian heresy continued to prosper. Not only did it find friends in the Empire, but it also won many converts among the barbarian tribes who were pouring into the empire and carving out chunks of it for themselves. Orthodox Catholic bishops often found themselves pitted against Arian secular authorities bent on increasing the influence of their sect.

4. *The importance of Scripture.* Some of the greatest scholars of Scripture come from this era, and we hear over and over how knowing the Scriptures is a key to the Christian life.

Representative Father

If you have time for only one of the Fathers in this group, read the audiences on **St. Jerome** (Chapter 21). It would be hard to overestimate his influence on the study of Scripture, and his famously difficult personality not only makes him an entertaining character to meet, but also raises fruitful questions about how we judge others.

In Practice

Think about your duty as a Christian citizen this week. Are we doing everything we can for the poor and neglected? Who really needs help? Is our government going in the right direction? What are we doing as citizens to push it in the right direction? Political and ethical issues are usually complicated, with no simple answers to the questions they bring up. But try thinking about them from a purely Christian point of view, and see whether that point of view brings any clarity.

More to Read

For more on this period in the history of the Church, read *The Fathers of the Church, Expanded Edition,* by Mike Aquilina, pages 176-177. See also *The Fathers* by Pope Benedict XVI, pages 129-174. (Both of these books are available from Our Sunday Visitor.)

CHAPTER 19

St. Ambrose of Milan

A towering figure in Church history and Christian thought, St. Ambrose is still even more famous for his influence on the great St. Augustine. It was Ambrose's gentle but powerful example that pushed Augustine toward his final conversion to Christianity.

Ambrose rose to prominence during the Arian controversies, when theological debates often turned into riots in the streets. As a civil magistrate, Ambrose had won the respect of both the Arian and the orthodox sides for his scrupulous fairness. When the Arian bishop of Milan died, the people — both Arian and Catholic — demanded Ambrose for their bishop, even though he had not even been baptized yet and was barely acquainted with Scripture.

He took on the job reluctantly, but when he realized there was no way out of it, he threw himself into it with rare enthusiasm. He gave up all his considerable possessions and studied Scripture tirelessly, eventually becoming one of history's greatest authorities on the Bible. He encouraged hymn-singing in church and wrote many of the hymns himself, and he was a tireless teacher.

Aside from his enormous influence on Augustine, Ambrose is probably best remembered for his strong distinction between church and state. He was obedient to the Emperor and the civil government in everything that was in their sphere, but he insisted that only the Church had the right to control its own administration and doctrine. When the Emperor insisted that he hand over a number of churches in the city to the Arians, Ambrose assembled large numbers of Catholic faithful and occupied the buildings until the Emperor relented. It was Ambrose more than anyone else who set the tone for the relationship between church and state in the West for the next thousand years.

Main Points

1. Ambrose died a memorably holy death on Holy Saturday, participating symbolically in Christ's crucifixion and resurrection.

2. Ambrose brought Origen's methods of studying Scripture to the Western Church.
3. His teaching began with reading Scripture in order to learn how to live a Christian life.
4. Once the catechumens had learned how to live as Christians, they were prepared to understand the mysteries of Christ.
5. Ambrose's intimate familiarity with Scripture deeply impressed St. Augustine.
6. For him, the true disciple is the one who knows Scripture so well that he can proclaim its message convincingly.

Questions for Reflection or Discussion

1. Why does the Holy Father begin the story of Ambrose's life with the story of his death?
2. How could a man who had not yet even been baptized possibly be qualified to be bishop? What could the people have seen in Ambrose's secular life that recommended him to them?
3. Why did Ambrose's teaching begin with the stories in the Old Testament?
4. Why was it so significant to Augustine that Ambrose could read Scripture without moving his lips?

CHAPTER 20

St. Maximus of Turin

As the Roman Empire continued to fall apart, leaders of the Church found themselves more and more forced to become leaders in civil society as well. St. Maximus of Turin is a good example. Barbarian raiders moved freely through the countryside, sending poor farmers to take refuge in now-walled cities. The civil government decayed into ineffectual dithering. Only the Church had any effective organization.

Yet even as the world seemed to be circling the drain, people who called themselves Christians could not contain their own greed, eagerly snapping up their neighbors' stolen goods and hoarding what riches they could accumulate without regard for the poor and destitute, of whom there were many more after the barbarian raids. St. Maximus directed his most famous preaching toward those who still had possessions, reminding them that a Christian must use his possessions to help those who have none. In this difficult situation, St. Maximus saw very clearly the link between being a good Christian and being a good citizen.

Main Points

1. Maximus worked to hold his city together at a time when barbarians threatened from outside and divisions from inside.
2. He preached to wealthy landowners, reminding them of their obligations to those less fortunate.
3. For Maximus, living a Christian life entails taking on civil duties as well. The good Christian must be a good citizen.
4. Maximus was compelled to take on secular leadership of the city as the government descended into chaos.

Questions for Reflection or Discussion

1. If the things of this world are only temporary, why do we need to worry about civic duty? Isn't that just a distraction from our real goal?

2. Maximus scolded his parishioners for buying goods looted from sacked cities. Do we do anything similar? Are there things we buy that encourage injustice in other parts of the world?
3. How should a good Christian participate in civic life today? What duties do we have to civil society?
4. Is it a good thing for the Church to be in charge of the civil government, or should that arrangement be a last resort in times of necessity?

CHAPTER 21

St. Jerome

Probably best known as the translator of the Bible, St. Jerome had a hot temper and was prone to ecclesiastical feuding. But he was also a brilliant scholar and one of the great lights of Christian literature.

Jerome grew up schooled in the best classical tradition — a schooling that would serve him well in later life, making him one of the most eloquent Christian writers. He had been headed for a career in government, but when he met some Christian hermits, he was so impressed with their way of life that he gave up everything and became a hermit himself. Eventually he ended up in the eastern deserts, where he spent his time studying Hebrew and Greek. His thorough knowledge of the original languages of Scripture made him a formidable interpreter of the Bible.

Jerome's most famous work was his revision of the Latin translation of the Bible, which was the basis for the Vulgate, the standard Latin version of Scripture in the Catholic Church even today. He also compiled a kind of biographical encyclopedia of the Church Fathers before his time, giving us one of our most valuable sources of information about early Christian history.

Jerome's personality is full of contradictions. His temper often came out in his writing, and he could be terribly difficult to get along with. On the other hand, he lived a life of exemplary self-denial and wrote some of the most insightful commentaries on Scripture ever put on paper. In the end, we have to take him with all his faults, because his virtues and accomplishments are so extraordinary.

PART 1. LIFE AND WRITINGS
Main Points

1. In studying Scripture, Jerome placed great importance on respecting the exact wording.
2. He insisted on referring to the original languages when interpretations of Scripture were in dispute.

3. In biblical commentaries, Jerome offered multiple interpretations, leaving the reader to judge between them.

4. Jerome admonished, "Ignorance of the Scriptures is ignorance of Christ."

5. We encounter the Word of God most fully in the Liturgy, where the Word is made present among us.

Questions for Reflection or Discussion

1. Most of us will never study Hebrew or Greek. How can we avoid misunderstanding Scripture when it's translated into English?

2. If there is only one Truth, how can there be multiple interpretations of a passage in Scripture?

3. St. Jerome's bad temper was notorious. How could someone so deficient in charity and patience still be remembered as a great Christian?

4. How can we deal with Christians who, like St. Jerome, have little tolerance for the faults of others?

PART 2. TEACHINGS

Main Points

1. God speaks to the faithful every day through Scripture.

2. A good Christian should read the Scriptures frequently, even constantly.

3. Prayer is necessary for understanding Scripture, because we always need the help of the Holy Spirit.

4. Scripture must always be read in harmony with the teaching of the Church, which alone can keep us from error.

5. Reading Scripture must go along with a truly Christian life.

6. Education was one of Jerome's primary interests, the purpose of education being to form a soul to become the temple of the Lord.

Questions for Reflection or Discussion

1. How can we find time in our busy lives to read Scripture more often?

2. Reading Scripture at home is a good thing. But how can we be sure we understand it according to the teaching of the Church?

3. Why was it so important to Jerome to be united to the see of St. Peter?

4. What habits do our children learn by observing us? Should we be worried about what they're learning?

CHAPTER 22

Aphraates, "the Sage"

Often known under the spelling "Aphrahat," Aphraates was a Persian bishop who addressed most of his surviving writings to Jews. The Jewish community in Persia at that time was prosperous and influential, whereas Christians were persecuted. Thus many of Aphraates' arguments attempt to show that the Christian religion is the true heir of the religion of the Old Testament. He concentrates on history rather than theology, because his opponents did not dispute the facts of Old Testament history.

Aphraates wrote in Syriac, a language closely related to the Aramaic spoken by Jesus and his disciples. Because his works were not in Greek or Latin, he has not been very well known in the West. But his fortunes have been changing recently, and scholars are beginning to appreciate this neglected Father of the East.

Main Points

1. Aphraates came from a world steeped in the Semitic traditions through which the Bible itself came.
2. The Christian community to which he belonged kept strong links to Jerusalem and the Jewish traditions.
3. Christian life, for Aphraates, is centered on the imitation of Christ.
4. Humility is essential, since humility actually raises us toward God.
5. Fasting and self-denial are important aspects of charity.

Questions for Reflection or Discussion

1. Why would Aphraates believe that humility is one of the most useful virtues?
2. How does humility bring us upward to God?
3. Why would Aphraates say that fasting is necessary in order to be charitable?
4. If fasting and self-denial are necessary, how can we say that the human body is good?

CHAPTER 23

St. Ephrem, the Syrian

The most important Syriac writer among the Fathers, St. Ephrem grew up in a Semitic culture not far different from the culture Jesus grew up in. Unlike most other Syriac writers, he became well known among Greek and Latin Christians, even in his own lifetime — partly owing to the place where he lived, a border town that frequently changed hands between the Roman and Persian Empires. Not much is known about his life, but many volumes of his writings have survived.

Of all the Fathers, Ephrem is probably the most profound poet. Others, like St. Ambrose, wrote memorable hymns and poetry, but most of Ephrem's output was poetical. He even wrote homilies in verse. In prose, he tended toward literal and historical interpretations of Scripture. But in verse, he gave free rein to allegory, and his striking imagery often clothes a deep and carefully worked-out theology. He is listed among the Doctors of the Church.

Main Points

1. St. Ephrem is the best-known Christian writer in Syriac.
2. Much of his writing is poetry; "he produces theology in poetical form."
3. He used striking contrasts and paradoxical images to teach profound truths of faith.
4. His hymns were meant to teach as they were sung.
5. Ephrem remained a deacon — a servant — to the end of his life.

Questions for Reflection or Discussion

1. Why would someone choose to write theology in verse?
2. Why would Ephrem think it was persuasive to use paradoxes — seemingly impossible contrasts — to illustrate truths of theology?
3. Why would Ephrem find poetry more conducive to allegory than prose?
4. Why does the Holy Father find it significant that Ephrem remained a deacon to the end of his life?

CHAPTER 24

St. Chromatius of Aquileia

Certainly one of the most obscure of the Fathers, St. Chromatius was Bishop of Aquileia, a city in what is today northeastern Italy, northeast of Venice. Aquileia was famous as a stronghold of orthodoxy in the Arian controversies, and Athanasius himself took refuge there during one of his frequent exiles. Chromatius grew up in a Christian family noted for piety and virtue, and he was ordained a bishop by St. Ambrose.

Most of his writings were lost until some were rediscovered relatively recently, which is one of the reasons for his relative obscurity. We now have a number of his homilies and commentaries on the Gospel of Matthew.

Barbarian attacks were a constant danger toward the end of Chromatius's life, and he probably died in exile while fleeing the invasions of northern Italy.

Main Points

1. Chromatius was raised in a Christian family and learned theology from a remarkable assortment of great minds who converged on Aquileia.
2. Constantly listening to the Word of God, Chromatius believed, is essential for being able to proclaim the message of the Gospel.
3. Christ's humanity was vitally important to him: he emphasized that Christ took on our humanity in totality.
4. The humanity of Christ led him to a keen appreciation of the importance of the Virgin Mary.
5. In spite of barbarian incursions, Chromatius did not lose his faith in God's protection.

Questions for Reflection or Discussion

1. Arians denied that Christ was equal to God the Father. Why, in the face of that heresy, was it important for Chromatius to emphasize that Christ was truly human?

2. How does remembering that Christ was truly human affect our view of Mary?
3. How might understanding the humanity of Christ be important for the unity of the Church?
4. When barbarians are at the gate, or even pouring through it, how is it possible to believe that God is protecting us?

CHAPTER 25

St. Paulinus of Nola

St. Paulinus was born in Bordeaux. It was an important intellectual center in late Roman times, and young Paulinus got the best classical education from a well-known pagan poet named Ausonius, with a view to a political career. Jolted out of his complacency by the death of his infant son, Paulinus gave up his career and — with the approval of his devoted Christian wife — all his worldly possessions, moving to Nola in southern Italy, a few miles inland from Naples. There his exemplary life persuaded the people to make him their bishop.

Paulinus wrote many letters to friends, of which some of the most memorable are his letters to his old teacher, Ausonius, which (of course) he wrote in verse. He was known as a saint in his own lifetime, but in addition his political skills made him a capable administrator, and he was responsible for building the basilica at Nola.

Main Points

1. For Paulinus worldly goods were not worthless, but instead worth more because they could be put to good use in caring for the poor.
2. In building the basilica of Nola, Paulinus specified that its decorations should teach the people who saw them.
3. Paulinus used his poetic talent to write many Christian hymns.
4. Friendship with other Christians was an important part of Paulinus's spiritual life.
5. For him, friendship was a manifestation of Christian unity.

Questions for Reflection or Discussion

1. What skills from our working lives could we apply to building up the Church?
2. What forms of art today might best help teach people about the message of the Gospel?

3. How does friendship enrich our spiritual lives?
4. Is friendship always a positive spiritual influence? How do we know what kind of friendship is truly beneficial?

St. Augustine

All the other Fathers of the Church take up one or two audiences at the most, but St. Augustine takes up five. What makes him so important?

To put it quite simply, Augustine was brilliant. A mind like his comes along once in centuries. He is one of the great figures of history, one of the great figures of theology, one of the great figures of philosophy, and one of the great figures of literature. To be one of those alone would be unusual enough, but to be all of those at once is almost unique. Augustine set the agenda in European thought for the next thousand years, and to a great extent Christians still rely on his thought.

But Augustine was also human, and the story of his long and twisting path to his ultimate conversion is one of the great Christian stories.

We probably know more about Augustine than we know about any other Church Father. Not only has he left us thousands of pages of theological writing, but he also wrote what may be the most widely read autobiography of all time: the *Confessions*. This remarkable book takes us through his early life in unflinching detail. He remembers all his sins, and he never spares us the embarrassing parts. The book is not just a window on Augustine's life, but also a detailed picture — perhaps the most detailed we have — of the western Roman Empire in its last days.

Augustine was born in North Africa in the year 354, about forty years after Constantine had made Christianity legal in the Empire. His father was a pagan bureaucrat; his mother Monica was a saintly Christian who raised him in the Christian faith. He went off to school in the big city — Carthage — at the age of sixteen, where, like many young men in college, he gradually fell away from the faith he had grown up in. He took a mistress, who bore him a son, and he indulged in every pleasure available to a young man of means.

One of his greatest pleasures was philosophy. He had an insatiable desire to know. He took up with the Manicheans, a dualistic heretical sect who believed that Creation was the product of an inferior deity, and at least halfheartedly joined them for several years. Meanwhile, he continued his studies and became a sought-after teacher of rhetoric.

He moved to Rome to try his luck at opening a school in the metropolis, but there was too much competition, and when a good job opened up in Milan, he took it. Now he was set, with good money, good friends, and everything it took to live the good life. He was rich and famous, and he ought to have been happy.

Yet he wasn't satisfied. Something was missing.

In Milan Augustine met Bishop Ambrose, a man whose intellect matched his own. But Ambrose was at peace and happy. With infinite patience, Ambrose slowly led Augustine back to the faith of his childhood, enjoying long philosophical conversations with him and never pushing him harder than he wanted to be pushed. In the year 387, Augustine came back to the Christian Church.

Eventually Augustine moved back to North Africa, where in 395 he became the Bishop of Hippo. He was a very active bishop, but he still found time to produce volumes and volumes of writing on every subject.

Meanwhile, the western half of the Roman Empire was falling apart. The sack of Rome in 410 hung over Augustine's thought for the rest of his life, and Augustine himself died in 430 as the barbarian Vandals were besieging his city of Hippo in North Africa. The impermanence of earthly wealth was emphasized with every barbarian attack. Augustine devoted his greatest work, the *City of God*, to the difference between the earthly and the heavenly.

The Dark Ages were falling, but Augustine was a beacon that would guide Christianity through the next ten centuries and into the present day. Among Western Christian theologians, only St. Thomas Aquinas is quoted as often as St. Augustine, and much of St. Thomas's work is based on the work of Augustine before him.

Important Themes

St. Augustine wrote on so many subjects that it's hard to pick out any particular themes as characteristic of his work. But some ideas were obviously important to him, because they come up over and over.

1. *The importance of grace.* It's dangerous to deny free will, but equally dangerous to deny the importance of God's grace. We have the ability to choose, but we can do nothing good without the help of God's grace, which is given freely to us.

St. Augustine developed much of his important thought on the subject of grace during the Pelagian controversy, in which the followers of Pelagius held that it was possible to be saved through human effort. If you tried reasonably hard to be good, you could make it to heaven. Augustine successfully argued that, although we do have free will, salvation is not possible without the grace of God.

2. *The Christian's home is in heaven.* The barbarian sack of Rome had proved that nothing, not even mighty Rome herself, was permanent on earth. As Christians, we belong to the City of God, which is our true home, and which alone lasts forever.

In Practice

Try to imagine telling the story of your life to God, the way St. Augustine did in his *Confessions.* How does it change your view of your own life, knowing that the Person you're talking to can see through any little distortions or lies you tell yourself? Does it help you see how God was acting in your life even when you weren't thinking about God?

More to Read

For more about St. Augustine, read *The Fathers of the Church, Expanded Edition*, by Mike Aquilina, pages 204-207. See also *The Fathers* by Pope Benedict XVI, pages 175-201. (Both of these books are available from Our Sunday Visitor.)

CHAPTER 26

St. Augustine of Hippo

PART 1. EARLY LIFE

Main Points

1. Augustine tapped the "intrinsic wealth" of Christianity, drawing ideas from that source that would shape the thought of future generations.

2. The pagan writer Cicero set Augustine off on his quest for wisdom, which would ultimately lead to his conversion.

3. At first, the Old Testament Scriptures did not seem to satisfy his hunger for wisdom.

4. With the help of Ambrose, Augustine came to see that the whole Old Testament is a journey toward Christ.

5. Although he had not felt called to be a pastor, when he was put in that position, he was tirelessly committed to pastoral work.

Questions for Reflection or Discussion

1. How is it possible to draw new ideas from a religion whose Scriptures and doctrines have already been established for centuries?

2. Why would Augustine count a pagan writer's work as the fist step on his journey to conversion? How is it possible for a non-Christian to lead us to Christian faith?

3. Think about the most recent Old Testament reading at Mass. How did it point toward Christ?

4. How many of us are doing what God has called us to do in our own careers and lives? Even if we don't feel as though God called us to our present work, have we done everything we can to make our work an instrument of the Gospel?

PART 2. LATER LIFE

Main Points

1. Augustine appointed a successor in his old age and retired to an astonishingly productive life of writing.
2. He was in his last illness when the Vandals besieged Hippo.
3. Augustine saw the troubles of the world as like the last illnesses of old age.
4. In Christ, he reminded his fellow citizens, our youth will be renewed.
5. In spite of his exemplary later life, Augustine spent his last days in repentance and prayer.

Questions for Reflection or Discussion

1. How could Augustine find hope even when his city was besieged and the world was apparently coming to an end?
2. Is our world once again in its old age, as the Roman Empire was? Or is the earthly world always in its old age when compared with the world to come?
3. Is old age a good metaphor for our spiritual state, even when we're physically young?
4. Why would someone as holy as Augustine need to repent? What does that say about us?

PART 3. TEACHINGS: FAITH AND REASON

Main Points

1. The relationship of faith and reason is a crucial point in understanding Augustine's life and work.
2. Faith is essential to understanding, but understanding is essential to stronger faith.
3. Because faith and reason are in harmony, God is close to us, even within us.
4. Because the Church is the Body of Christ, no one can be saved outside the Church.

Questions for Reflection or Discussion

1. Why is faith essential to understanding? How can we believe before we understand?
2. If understanding is essential to faith, what should we be trying to understand? How do we go about understanding?
3. How does reason help us find God within ourselves?
4. Why is it important to understand that our nature is social?

PART 4. WRITINGS

Main Points

1. Augustine's literary output was huge, with more than a thousand works published.
2. Augustine wrote his own life as a dialogue with God.
3. Late in his life, Augustine set an example of intellectual humility by going through his works and pointing out his own faults.
4. The *City of God*, written in reaction to the sack of Rome in 410, presents all of history in terms of the struggle between love of self and love of God.
5. Although he was a profound theologian, it was more important to Augustine to be able to teach the many.

Questions for Reflection or Discussion

1. Why is humility an important intellectual virtue?
2. Why would the story of his own life and experience be the best-known work of one of Christianity's most profound thinkers?
3. How does Augustine's life fit the pattern of the struggle between love of self and love of God?
4. How might we follow Augustine's example of bringing Christian theology to ordinary people without watering down the truth?

PART 5. THE TRIPLE CONVERSION

Main Points

1. Augustine's conversion was not accomplished all at once; it was a long journey.

2. That journey continued to the end of his life.

3. In spite of his straying from the Church, philosophy ultimately brought Augustine closer to Christ.

4. Pope Benedict sees three conversions in Augustine's life: his initial giving himself up to Christ, his realization that simplicity and humility are what spread the Gospel, and his final understanding that we need constant renewal from Christ.

Questions for Reflection or Discussion

1. Have you had one outstanding conversion experience? Or has your life been more of a continuous journey?

2. Augustine's conversion was still going on to the end of his life. What kinds of conversion might we still need to go through?

3. Classical philosophy brought Augustine closer to God. Can the secular knowledge we pick up today in schools and universities still do the same for us?

4. How could we — individually or together in our church — improve in simplicity and humility?

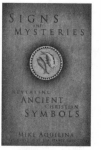

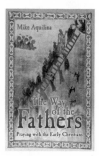